The 500 Hidden Secrets of

VALENCIA

INTRODUCTION

This guide book takes a fresh look at Valencia and helps visitors find their way to the heart of the city. It's filled with carefully curated lists that take people off the beaten track, towards tucked away and inspiring places.

The 500 Hidden Secrets of Valencia zooms in on the coolest neighbourhoods, from buzzy Russafa with its pioneering galleries and maverick bars to beach-side Cabanyal with its powerful community and beautifully tiled fisherman's houses.

It features an enviable address book of must-visit bars and restaurants. Find out where the locals go for paella, which beach shacks host the wildest parties and where to find neighbourhood bodegas where the wine is poured straight from the barrel.

Dive into festivals and local history, like fiery Fallas where people party for days and fireworks whizz and crackle down every street. Find out why *almuerzo* – brunch's boozy older sibling – is the must-try breakfast in the city, discover the fascinating stories behind Valencia's most characterful buildings, and swot up on some haunting local myths and legends.

The guide also reveals brilliant weekend plans, from rural wineries with bedrooms among the vineyards to secluded waterfalls and wild swimming spots.

THE AUTHOR

Lucy Lovell lives in Valencia and works as a freelance writer covering travel, food and drink for publications around the world.

Her move to Spain was sparked by promises of adventures in a VW camper from her long-distance partner, and in 2020 she took the leap. They now live together in the old town of Valencia with their two children, Sebastian and Rafael.

Lucy has compiled an eclectic list of places old and new. For her it is important to shine a light on the time-warp bodegas just as much as the shiny new cafes. Valencia is wonderfully skilled at weaving tradition and heritage into new projects, something that this book has tried very hard to honour.

With Seb in nursery, Lucy went to lots of these places with baby Rafy on her hip, and wants to thank him for being so amiable during these trips. She would also like to thank her partner Richard for pouring in countless hours of childcare (and glasses of vermouth) to help her. Thanks are also due to Maje for her valued advice, to Sarah for her cocktail prowess, to Silvia for her design expertise, and to Ana and Monica for their excellent dance moves.

The author would also like to thank Dettie from Luster for her guidance in compiling this book and Paula for the perfect pictures.

Finally, she would like to thank the much-loved JP for first introducing her to this beautiful city.

HOW TO
USE THIS BOOK

This guide lists 500 things you need to know about Valencia in 100 different categories. Most of these are places to visit, with practical information to help you find your way. Others are bits of information that help you get to know the city and its habitants. The aim of this guide is to inspire, not to cover the city from A to Z.

The places listed in the guide are given an address, including the neighbourhood, and a number. The neighbourhood and number allow you to find the locations on the maps at the beginning of the book: first look for the map of the corresponding neighbourhood, then look for the right number. A word of caution: these maps are not detailed enough to allow you to find specific locations in the city. You can locate (and pin) the addresses on your smartphone and you can always obtain an excellent map from any tourist office or in most hotels.

Please also bear in mind that cities change all the time. The chef who hits a high note one day may be uninspiring on the day you happen to visit. The hotel ecstatically reviewed in this book might suddenly go downhill under a new manager. Or the bar considered one of the '5 coolest craft beer bars' might be empty on the night you visit. This is obviously a highly personal selection. You might not always agree with it. If you want to leave a comment, recommend a bar or reveal your favourite secret place, please visit the website *the500hiddensecrets.com* – you'll also find a lot of free tips and the latest news on the series there – or follow @500hiddensecrets on Instagram or Facebook and leave a comment.

DOWNLOAD
TWO FREE WALKS

Next to selecting 500 hidden secrets in Valencia, author Lucy Lovell
has also mapped out two city walks. These walks are a great way
to explore two of the most interesting and bustling areas in Valencia
and will lead you past several of the addresses in the book. The walks
are available as digital downloads in the *500hiddensecrets.com* webshop.
As the owner of this book, you get them for free by scanning the
QR code below:

VALENCIA

overview

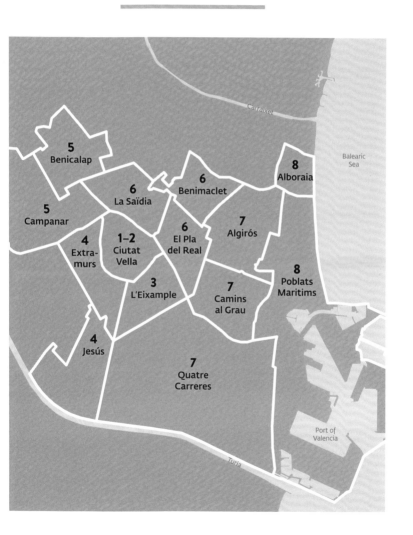

Map 1
CIUTAT VELLA
(NORTH)

Map 2
CIUTAT VELLA
(SOUTH)

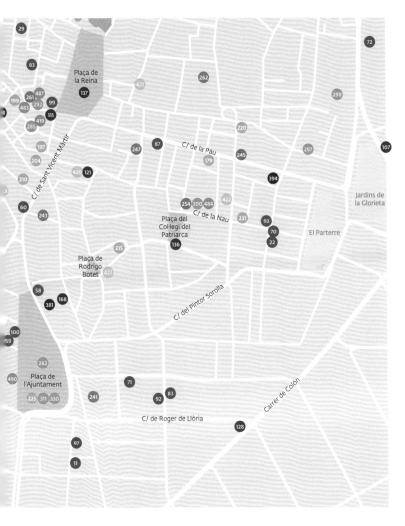

Map 3
L'EIXAMPLE

Jardins de l'Antic Hospital

Plaça de l'Ajuntament

C/ de Xàtiva

Carrer de Colón

420

Gran Via de Ramón y Cajal

València Nord

Plaça de Bous de València

205

C/ de Ciril Amorós

242
493

Gran Via del Marqués del Túr

175

Av. del Regne de València

246

164

230

Gran Via de les Germanies

391

94

178

339

183

180

73

154

21

190

335

380

228

112

Mercat de Russafa

437

8

62

C/ de Cadis

450

181

C/ de Cuba

332

218 39 149

C/ de Puerto Rico

333

6

345

108

157

334

44 117

43

331

42

119

202

Carrer del Literat Azorín

182

València Joaquín Sorolla

191

192

395 156

417

275

Map 4
EXTRAMURS *and* JESÚS

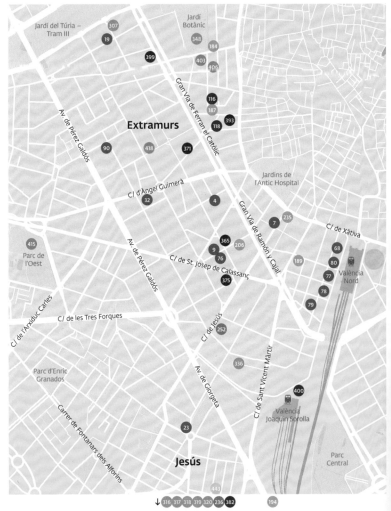

Map 5
BENICALAP *and* CAMPANAR

EAT — **DRINK** — SHOP — BUILDINGS — DISCOVER — **CULTURE** — CHILDREN — SLEEP — **WEEKEND** — RANDOM

Map 6
LA SAÏDIA, BENIMACLET
and EL PLA DEL REAL

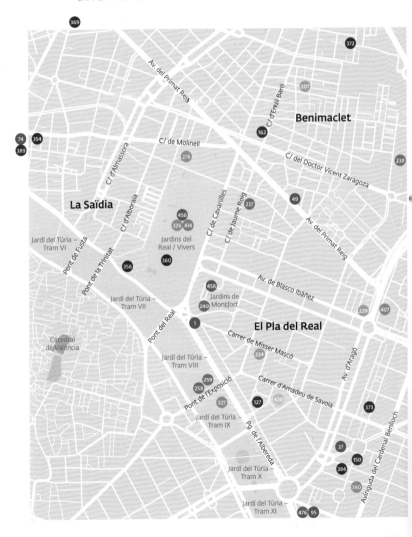

EAT — **DRINK** — SHOP — BUILDINGS — DISCOVER — **CULTURE** — CHILDREN — SLEEP — WEEKEND — RANDOM

Map 7
ALGIRÓS, CAMINS AL GRAU
and QUATRE CARRERES

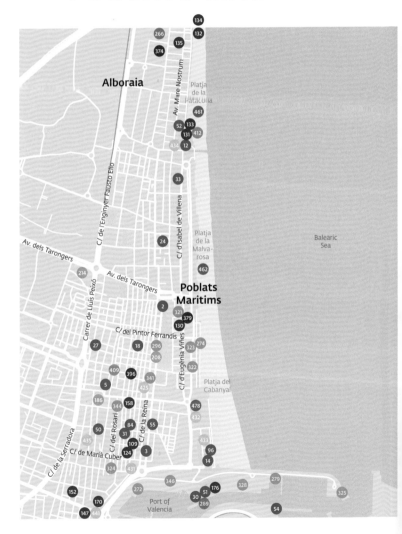

Map 8

ALBORAIA *and*

POBLATS MARITIMS

134
132
266
135
374

Alboraia

Platja
de la
Patacona

461
52 133
131 412
434 12

33

C/ d'Isabel de Villena

24

Platja
de la
Malva-
rosa

462

Av. dels Tarongers

214

Av. dels Tarongers

Poblats
Maritims

Carrer de Lluís Peixó

2

321
379
130

C/ del Pintor Ferrandis

18 296
208

27

274

C/ d'Eugènia Viñes

323

322

409 396
341

5

425

Platja del
Cabanyal

186

344 158

478

432

50

84
31 55

C/ del Rosari

C/ de la Reina

124
109 3

C/ de Marià Cuber

433

96

14

C/ de la Serradora

435

324 431

346

272

51 176
30 269

328

279

325

152

170

147 441

Port of
Valencia

54

Balearic
Sea

Av. de l'Enginyer Fausto Elío

Av. Mare Nostrum

105 PLACES
TO EAT

The 5 best
ALMUERZO *joints*

1 **LA PÉRGOLA**
   Passeig de
   l'Albereda 1
   El Pla del Real ⑥
   +34 963 69 90 79

After breakfast and before lunch there is *almuerzo*: a hearty, cheap meal historically eaten by labourers before a hard day's work. La Pérgola is an A-lister; the red-capped kiosk has been slinging *bocadillos* since 1962. Order the *Súper Bombón*: a cotton-soft baguette filled with pork loin, cheese and an unholy amount of chips.

2 BODEGA LA PASCUALA

C/ del Doctor
Lluch 299
Poblats Maritims ⑧
+34 963 71 38 14
bodegalapascuala.es

La Pascuala's new home looks shiny and new, but they've brought over 100 years of *almuerzo* expertise with them from their old tavern (their former home was an old fisherman's guild, just a few hundred metres away). They are pioneers of the XL: *bocadillos* so big you could paddle out to sea in them.

3 CA RAKEL

C/ del Doctor
Lluch 9
Poblats Maritims ⑧
+34 664 29 06 31

Raquel fell in love with Valencia after visiting from Venezuela, and opened Ca Rakel in 2016. Sandwiches are big, messy and imaginative. Find hot takes on classics, like horse meat with gorgonzola and honey, or sirloin with silky foie gras sauce. Down-to-earth yet indulgent.

4 NUEVO OSLO BAR

C/ del Doctor
Sanchis Sivera 7
Extramurs ④
+34 963 85 04 93

Owner Raúl is so confident that he's the king of *almuerzo* he dishes out plastic crowns. Pop one on and order a Quart de Poblet with homemade *figatells* (made with pork meat, liver and kidneys) caramelised onions and chewy baguette. Finish on a punchy *cremaet* to put a skip in your step.

5 BODEGA BAR FLOR

C/ Marti Grajales 21
Poblats Maritims ⑧
+34 963 71 20 19
*restaurante
bodegaflor.es*

Third-generation run and always full, this bar hasn't changed much since it opened in 1893. Wine and soda is the preferred drink and the house special (it doesn't have a name – ask for the *especialidad de la casa*), made with chips, gravy and sausages, is one of the best in the city.

5 brilliant places for
BRUNCH

---

6 **BLACKBIRD CAFÉ**
C/ de la Reina
Na Maria 7
L'Eixample ③
+34 960 05 10 90

Spot busy bakers through the kitchen's huge glass window; they're whipping up some of the best cakes around, from croissants crammed with velvety pistachio cream to brownies topped with lime and mascarpone. Classic brunch plates like avocado on toast are dolled up with feta, cherry tomatoes and crispy bacon.

7 **CASA CAPICÚA**
C/ de Jesús 14
Extramurs ④
+34 611 62 24 23
casacapicua.es

The first venture by twin sisters Marta and Laura Benito, Casa Capicúa serves a modern Mediterranean take on brunch. Eggs are shunned in favour of toast with avocado and peppery olive oil, or roast chicken with pickles on springy buns. Local ceramicist Adriana Cabello made the gorgeous coffee cups.

8   BLUEBELL COFFEE

C/ de Buenos Aires 3
L'Eixample ③
+34 678 36 16 15
bluebellcoffeeco.com

Bluebell's brunch menu is zippy and light, with pops of bright pickles and greens. Coffee is roasted by owners Yolanda and Marian Valero: big players in Valencia's coffee scene who source brilliant beans from around the world. Dine outdoors in the sun-soaked, leafy courtyard in the summer.

9   FOUR COFFEE & BISTRO

C/ de l'Historiador Diago 20
Extramurs ④
+34 623 38 43 25
fourcoffeebistro.com

FOUR takes brunch to dizzy new heights with clever cooking and seasonal produce. Fat doughnuts, bagels speckled with sesame seeds and squidgy brioche are all made in-house. There's usually an eggs Benedict with unexpected toppings, like Black Angus roast beef or panko-breaded langoustines.

10   BRUNCH CORNER – LA VIRGEN

C/ del Comte d'Almodóvar 1
Ciutat Vella ①
+34 963 91 52 30
brunchcorner.es

Enormous Americana brunch deals are Brunch Corner's speciality. The All American tops the lot: pancakes with bacon, sausages, scrambled eggs and maple syrup – it even comes with a coffee, orange juice and a slab of cake. No tables at the La Virgen venue? Head to the peaceful terrace of the Sant Bult cafe – it's usually quieter.

5 **PAELLA** *spots*
loved by locals

---

11 **CASA BALDO 1915**
C/ de Ribera 5
Ciutat Vella ②
+34 960 81 57 29
grupogastrotrinquet.com/
restaurantes/casa-baldo

One word: *socarrat*. Casa Baldo absolutely nails that crispy layer of rice at the bottom of the pan. Paella Valenciana is a speciality, but they serve a stellar *arroz del senyoret*. Translated as 'gentleman's rice', the prawns come peeled and in bite-size pieces, so no messy fingers.

12 RESTAURANTE LLEVANT

Paseo Marítimo
de la Patacona 2
Alboraia ⑧
+34 963 56 44 85
*restaurantellevant
web.es*

It's not the prettiest spot on the seafront, but this no-frills restaurant is an institution. Llevant has been serving *arroz a leña* (rice cooked over fire) since 1907, and in-the-know diners order *arroz negro* (licorice-black rice with squid in its own ink) to go with their sea views. Booking advised, especially on Sundays.

13 GOYA GALLERY

C/ de Borriana 3
L'Eixample ③
+34 963 04 18 35
*goyagallery
restaurant.com*

Reception might seem a bit snooty, but it's forgiven when the paella is this good. Inside, a marble bust shows off gold medals which they bagged at local paella competitions. *Afficianados* cringe at a pan overfilled with stodgy rice; here it's wafer thin, and even the *senyoret* is never too salty.

14 LA PEPICA

Passeig de Neptú 6
Poblats Maritims ⑧
+34 963 71 03 66
lapepica.com

This iconic restaurant is known for its famous fans, like Hemingway and Orson Welles. They too have followed the red velvet rope past lobsters on ice and a ferocious kitchen where flames lick pans of bubbling rice. *Paella Pepica* is the one, sprinkled with perfectly cooked seafood. Tip: book the terrace for beach views.

15 LA BARRACA DE TONI MONTOLIU

Partida de l'Ermita 25
Meliana
+34 603 73 37 14
*barracatoni
montoliu.com*

A *barraca* is a traditional Valencian farmhouse, and the 20-minute drive to Toni's is so worth it. Loaded with home-grown produce, the paella is eaten outside under the shade of trees or indoors where walls are decorated with straw hats and pitchforks. Finish with a bumpy jaunt in the horse-drawn carriage.

5 old-school
TAPAS BARS

16 **MAIPI**
C/ del Mestre Josep
Serrano 1
L'Eixample ③
+34 963 73 57 09
maipi.es

Gambas on ice, platters of marbled
beef and blushing Valencian tomatoes;
Maipi's spread has been chosen by owner
Gabi Serrano and his wife Pilar Costa
at the market that morning for their
freshness and quality. Perch at the bar
and scoff butter-soft roasted lamb or
slow-cooked oxtail.

17 **BOATELLA TAPAS**
Plaça del Mercat 34
Ciutat Vella ②
+34 963 15 40 71
boatellatapas.es

Boatella Tapas is a lively spot with lovely
views of Mercat Central from the terrace.
A motley clientele of locals and visitors
enjoy the brusque brand of service from
waiters, who rush around with seasonal
delicacies like crispy fried artichokes and
tellinas like buttery popcorn.

19 BAR RICARDO

18 BODEGA LA ALDEANA 1927

C/ de Josep
Benlliure 258
Poblats Maritims ⑧
+34 644 75 26 12
*bodegalaaldeana1927.
eatbu.com*

Behind the polished beachfront bars is this much-loved local, where friends toast with glasses of Alhambra over plates of fat olives, sticky fig *marmalade* with *morcilla*, and *patatas bravas* with a fierce *aioli*. *Almuerzo* is popular, too; half a *bocadillo* and a drink will set you back under 6 euro.

19 BAR RICARDO

C/ del Doctor
Zamenhof 16
Extramurs ④
+34 963 82 37 89
barricardo.es

The bar is the best seat here; diners find themselves eye-to-eye with fresh lobsters and *gambas rayadas* (the world's most delicious and hard-to-catch prawns) while they sip a chilled cava. Is it cheap? Heck no, but the menu is impeccably prepared. Some say their *patatas bravas* is the best in Valencia.

20 RESTAURANTE JM

C/ de Pere
Aleixandre 38
Quatre Carreres ⑦
+34 963 73 95 32
restaurantejm.com

Tables dressed in paper tablecloths are hot property at Restaurante JM: locals bicker for the last one while googly-eyed fish watch from the cabinets and spaghetti westerns play on the TV. Grab a quick tapa of *esgarraet* or go all out with French oysters, goose barnacles and rockfish fresh from the market.

5 cosy
NEIGHBOURHOOD GEMS

---

21 **LA TAULA DE YOON**
C/ del Doctor
Serrano 19
L'Eixample ③
+34 640 84 89 35

This cosy Korean restaurant is wall-to-wall big flavours. Spot owner Haesung Yoon in the kitchen while her partner Raúl runs front-of-house. The menu is concise: dumplings (like homemade kimchi and pork) or a handful of mains, like slow-cooked pork belly with *banchan* and lettuce leaves.

22 **OSTRAS PEDRÍN**
C/ de Bonaire 23
Ciutat Vella ②
+34 963 76 70 54
ostraspedrin.es

A stylish crowd head to Ostras Pedrín for a light dinner of seafood and cava. Pull up a stool and choose from a sea of craggy oysters: Valencian, Galician or Asturian, topped with your choice of caviar, spicy vinaigrette or lemon. The delicately smoked eel is a real treat too.

23 **EL OBSERVATORIO**
C/ de Jeroni
Munyós 15
Jesús ④
+34 960 80 77 52
elobservato riodepatraix.com

This low-key restaurant has gained a cult following for its modern, casual cooking with a dash of Nikkei. Don't be put off by the signage: it is not a *droguería*. On sunny mornings they fling open the windows and serve waffles with blueberries, and when the sun sets it's tangy ceviche, *gyozas* with *katsuobushi* and *pisco sours*.

24 **A FUEGO LENTO**
Plaça del Llibertador
Simón Bolívar 7
Poblats Maritims ⑧
+34 651 67 01 60

Hidden in an unfashionable square between blocks of high-rise flats, A Fuego Lento serves unfussy, market-fresh seafood. A daily changing menu might include calamari served in its own ink or grilled razor clams. Some dishes are gnarly, like the enormous roasted fish head: all the more reason to love them.

25 **ULTRAMARINOS HUERTA**
C/ del Mestre
Gozalbo 13
L'Eixample ③
+34 963 92 92 74
ultramarinoshuerta.com

This relaxed bistro serves souped-up versions of Spanish classics. Inside, find terracotta floors, traditional tiles and banquette seating where diners feast on squid *figatells*, confit artichokes, *huevos rotos* with runny yolks and tuna. The menu is long but it's all excellent – order as much as possible.

22 OSTRAS PEDRÍN

5 dreamy places to
DINE OUTDOORS

---

26 **ESCALONES DE LA LONJA**
C/ Pere Compte 3
Ciutat Vella ②

This trusty tapas bar could not be better located: opposite Mercat Central and wedged next to the Gothic architecture of La Lonja. Nibble on smokey *pimiento de padrón* (watch out for the spicy one), *bravas* and grilled steak with crunchy sea salt while you spot gargoyles on the roof across the street.

27 **FUMIFERRO**
C/ de Vicent
Ballester 38
Poblats Maritims ⑧
+34 960 72 66 40
fumiferro.com

Festoon lighting, mad graffiti and DJs make this suntrap terrace in Cabanyal a cool place to hang out. T-bone steaks and honey-glazed pork ribs are cooked over the grill, and sweet-toothed folks will love the lightly smoked cheesecake, still gooey in the middle.

28 TABERNA PARAISO TRAVEL
C/ de la Carda 6
Ciutat Vella ①
+34 691 54 92 09
juniorfranco.es/
paraiso-travel

Painted with enormous toucans and tropical cityscapes, the courtyard at Taberna Paraiso Travel is almost as colourful as the food. Chef Junior Franco serves playful plates with influences from around the world; their Colombian *arepa* with steak tartar is legendary.

29 BAR & KITCHEN
Plaça d'Ibanyes 7
Ciutat Vella ②
+34 961 488 717
mercadodetapineria.
com/bar-and-kitchen

It would be easy to spend all day in this bunting-lined square. The breakfast menu of toast with avocado and smoked salmon leads quite nicely into a casual all-day menu ('till 11:30 pm) of *bravas*, chicken wings and nachos with guacamole. On Sunday they make paella, but when it's gone it's gone.

30 LA MARÍTIMA
AT: VELES E VENTS
C/ Marina Real
Juan Carlos I
Poblats Maritims ⑧
+34 690 70 52 16
veleseventsvalencia.es/
restaurante/restaurante-
la-maritima

Just five minutes from the crowded beach, La Marítima's terrace is a calm waterside escape, where dapper diners watch sailboats mooring on the pier. It's on the ground floor of the Veles e Vents building, and chefs work wonders with fresh produce. Try the *gamba roja* for a sweet, briny hit.

5 charming
OLD RESTAURANTS

---

31 CASA MONTAÑA
C/ de Josep
Benlliure 69
Poblats Maritim ⑧
+34 963 67 23 14
emilianobodega.com

Founded in 1836, Casa Montaña is a charmer. Antique cabinets preserve old bottles of liquor and giant oak barrels are chalked up with the day's wine list. There's a more formal dining room at the back, but the bar is better. Dine on anchovies from Santoña and chorizo from Zamora.

32 RAUSELL
C/ d'Àngel
Guimerà 61
Extramurs ④
+34 963 84 31 93
rausell.es

Don't be fooled by Rausell's polished interior – it's not dripping in old world charm but it is a cultural cornerstone. Dating back to 1948, the third-generation run bistro serves first class seafood and deluxe rice dishes, like lobster, or baby squid with porcini mushrooms.

33 CASA CARMELA

C/ d'Isabel de
Villena 155
Poblats Maritims ⑧
+34 963 71 00 73
casa-carmela.com

From its origins as a changing room for beachgoers in the 1920's, Casa Carmela has bloomed into a gorgeously tiled cathedral to paella. Fourth-generation owner Toni Novo is a perfectionist. Don't miss out on excellently prepared starters, like fat Valencian oysters and grilled octopus.

34 EL RACÓ DE LA PAELLA

C/ de Mossèn
Rausell 17
Campanar ⑤
+34 963 48 82 52
elracodelapaella.es

Frescoes of *pueblo* life, ornate tiles and wobbly beams all date back to the 1890s, when this Valencian house was built. The restaurant arrived more recently, but the food is traditional. Paella is cooked over open fire (duck is the secret ingredient) and *torrijas* come served with *horchata* ice cream.

35 LA PILARETA

C/ del Moro Zeid 13
Ciutat Vella ①
+34 963 91 04 97
barlapilareta.es

La Pilareta's location in the heart of El Carmen, together with its charming decor, sassy service and affordable dishes, makes for a pretty outstanding spot. *Clotxinas* – a small, sweet type of mussel – are their speciality. Do as the locals do and chuck the empty shells in the buckets on the floor.

5 amazing
JAPANESE
RESTAURANTS

---

36 **NOZOMI SUSHI BAR**
C/ de Pere III
el Gran 11
L'Eixample ③
+34 961 48 77 64
nozomisushibar.es

You can hear a pin drop in the zen dining room of Nozomi, where laser-focussed chefs work to produce exquisite plates, from roasted tomato *dashi* to melt-in-the-mouth grilled wagyu. Look up at the pretty paper petals suspended from the ceiling, like a flurry of cherry blossom.

36 NOZOMI SUSHI BAR

37 KAIDO

C/ de Xile 3
El Pla del Real ⑥
+34 687 00 06 96
kaidosushi.es

Only ten people are allowed in at a time to this Michelin-starred restaurant. They are hypnotised by Yoshikazu Yanome as he masterfully prepares nigiri by hand and scorches fresh salmon with white-hot coals. Every ingredient is handled with care and expertise – right down to the last grain of sushi rice.

38 TABERNA TORA

C/ de Pere III
el Gran 13
L'Eixample ③
+34 963 11 94 29

Casual and affordable, Tora is a neat (and very popular) option for big plates like *yakisoba* loaded with crunchy veg and nibbles, like *takoyaki* with dancing *katsuobushi*, *gyoza* with crispy bottoms and chicken *karaage* with a craggy, shattering crust. Get here early at peak times, it's first come first served.

39 HIKARI YAKITORI BAR

C/ dels Tomasos 18
L'Eixample ③
+34 963 33 99 57
hikariyakitoribar.es

This informal spot is inspired by the *yakitori* bars of Tokyo's backstreets with neon lights, paper lanterns and corrugated iron. Book a seat at the bar to watch chefs diligently grilling skewers of sticky-sweet octopus, eel and heart over coal. How many should you order? Less is more; they're surprisingly filling.

40 SUSHI CRU

C/ del Pintor
Zariñena 3
Ciutat Vella ①
+34 963 92 54 92

For over 20 years this homely joint has been serving no-frills Japanese food. Dig into plates of *shashimi* with octopus, salmon and *wakame*, *udon* soup with seasonal vegetables, and neat salmon and avocado *maki*. No fish? No problem – vegans will be very well fed here.

5 restaurants that
V E G G I E S *will love*

---

41 LA LLUNA
C/ de Sant Ramon 23
Ciutat Vella ①
+34 963 92 21 46
restaurantelalluna.com

Everyone from cosy couples to rushed office workers seek out La Lluna for hearty veggie grub. It opened in 1980, and was the first vegetarian restaurant in Valencia. Flavours are a little dated (expect very well-cooked veggies and underwhelming soup) but don't let that put you off: it is a relic to be treasured.

42 LA CASA VIVA
C/ de Cadis 76
L'Eixample ③
+34 963 03 47 13
lacasaviva.com

You can tell that La Casa Viva is committed to the environment: even the plaster on the walls is ecologically sound. Wholesome dishes include yam chips (apparently they're better for you than potatoes) served with homemade tomato sauce and falafels made with brown rice and kale.

43 CAFÉ MADRIGAL
C/ de Puerto Rico 41
L'Eixample ③
+34 963 01 87 35
madrigal.cafe

Everything is vegan in this coffee, brunch and dinner spot in Russafa, even the tortilla, made with chickpea flour. It's so good it could give the original a run for its money. The small spot serves red chickpea curry, avocado bowls with edamame beans and lentil burgers with a clever cashew mayo.

44 COPENHAGEN

C/ del Literat
Azorín 8
L'Eixample ③
+34 963 28 99 28
grupocopenhagen.com

This restaurant group has three sites around the city; Copenhagen is their flagship. With minimal white walls, shelves stacked with wine and colourful art, it feels like going to your arty friend's house for a dinner party. Groups have animated conversations over bowls of gazpacho and genuinely delicious salads.

45 KUKLA

C/ de Palomino 8
Ciutat Vella ①
+34 665 47 90 38
kuklavalencia.com

Found on a graffiti-covered backstreet of El Carmen and styled like a kitsch living room, Kukla serves Middle Eastern food using co-owner Ronen's grandma's recipes as a starting point. Everything is delicious: hummus with lashings of *tahini*, emerald-green falafel and pita breads as fluffy as candy floss.

45 KUKLA

5 spots for extraordinary
CROQUETAS

---

46 CENTRAL BAR
AT: MERCAT CENTRAL DE
VALÈNCIA, PUESTO 105-112
**Plaça de la Ciutat
de Bruges
Ciutat Vella** ②
+34 963 82 92 23
centralbar.es

It's hard to overhype Central Bar, the informal joint of Valencian restaurateur Ricard Camarena, whose eponymous restaurant holds two Michelin stars. Take a seat among the peaches and olives of Mercat Central and ask for *croquetas de pollo rustido*; they're crispier than a Dorito and stuffed with a creamy roast chicken filling.

47 LOS MADRILES
**Av. del Regne
de València 48
L'Eixample** ③
+34 963 73 91 01
losmadrilestaberna.es

This modern *taberna* takes a new look at traditional Valencian food, and serves it in a modern bar with a touch of nostalgia. Their rugged *croquetas* are the colour of burnt caramel, the crisp outside hides fillings like *cocido* (a stew with meat and chickpeas) and Idiazabal sheep's cheese and truffle.

48 BAR MARVI
**C/ dels Sants Just
i Pastor 14
Camins al Grau** ⑦
+34 963 61 85 56
barmarvi.com

Opened in 1990, this bar has near-mythical status for its dedication to quality. The founders are originally from Galicia, hence the heavy lean on northern Spanish fare. Textbook *croquetas*, long and golden brown, might have robust fillings like oxtail and curry.

49 EL APRENDIZ

Plaça del Riu Duero 6
Benimaclet ⑥
+34 963 70 55 14
elaprendiztapas.com

In an unexpected corner of Benimaclet, El Aprendiz entices visitors with its clever menu and minimal interior. Here, *croquetas* get a Thai twist with mussels and a green curry sauce wrapped with a crispy-crackly crumb and a sweet tomato sauce. Thirsty? Homemade vermouth comes loaded with olives, orange and cinnamon.

50 BODEGA ANYORA

C/ d'En Vicent
Gallart 15
Poblats Maritims ⑧
+34 963 55 88 09
anyora.es

The canny owners of Anyora have revived this antique bar with a sophisticated touch. Decor looks back fondly on classic *bodegas*; there's a marble bar with dried garlic hanging overhead and rustic hand-painted murals. The menu is better than most in Cabanyal and their *croquetas* are made with *jamón ibérico*.

50 **BODEGA ANYORA**

5 lovely restaurants
NEAR THE WATER

---

51 LA SUCURSAL
AT: VELES E VENTS
C/ Marina Real
Juan Carlos I
Poblats Maritims ⑧
+34 96 374 66 65
*veleseventsvalencia.es/
restaurante/restaurante-
la-sucursal*

Perched on the top floor of the Veles e Vents building, La Sucursal's sleek dining room offers the most incredible views over the port. Head chef Fran Espí prods and probes ingredients to find brilliant new ways to serve them. Find sharp dishes like oysters with fermented oranges or glassy squid with charcoal oil.

52 LA MÁS BONITA
Passeig Marítim de
la Patacona 11
Alboraia ⑧
+34 963 14 36 11
*lamasbonita.es/en/
restaurants/patacona*

This boho hang-out is one of the best spots on the beach, but it also boasts the biggest queues. Need some menu inspo while you wait? Their club sandwich with a side of chips always goes down well after a morning splashing in the sea. And the *chocorgasmo* cake, although embarrassing to order, is utterly delicious.

53 RESTAURANTE L'ESTABLIMENT

Camino de l'Estell
El Palmar
+34 961 62 01 00
establiment.com

On Sundays, locals drive south to the Albufera for a peaceful paella, and many say L'Establiment serves the best. Spot herons and ospreys from the table, where emerald green water is so close you can almost dip your fingers in it. Reserve on the terrace to avoid the stuffy indoor dining room.

54 EL FARO DEL SUR

AT: MARINA SUR
C/ Marina Real
Juan Carlos I
Poblats Maritims ⑧
+34 695 30 71 77

Restaurants on the marina tend to be a bit flashy, but this no-frills shack hidden in the south marina is where boat owners come for a peaceful pint. The menu is basic; burgers with chips, beer and cocktails. It's a trek from the main drag, but the reward is a quiet terrace and marina views.

55 FESTINAR

C/ del Doctor
Lluch 46
Poblats Maritims ⑧
+34 623 02 20 77

People looking to dodge the beach crowds head to Festinar, a casual pizza restaurant in Cabanyal where you can't choose your toppings, but they're all pretty delicious. It's the sister site of Finestra in Russafa, and they're similarly hell-bent on good vibes, local community, and locally-sourced ingredients.

5 places to feast on
JAMÓN

56 **SOLAZ**
AT: MERCAT CENTRAL DE
VALÈNCIA, PUESTO 59-64
**Plaça de la Ciutat
de Bruges
Ciutat Vella ②
+34 963 82 92 05**

This stall in Mercat Central is stuffed with goodies, from raw goat's milk cheese from the Parque Natural de la Sierra to 25-day-matured truffle sheep's cheese from Segovia. Owner Paco Solaz loves *jamón*: he even collaborated with a producer in Trevélez to make his own, matured for 30 months with 2% salt.

57 EL HOGAR DEL IBÉRICO

C/ de la Reina
Na Germana 25
L'Eixample ③
+34 960 04 05 28

Jesús is the owner of this deli-cafe, and he's been trained in the art of *jamón* slicing. He has an encyclopaedic knowledge of the stuff. Pull up a stool at one of their old wine barrels, order a bottle of beer, and taste the difference between Duroc and 100% *pata negra jamón*.

58 BEHER

Plaça de
l'Ajuntament 16
Ciutat Vella ②
+34 961 02 07 93
beherstores.com/
valencia.html

As well as a huge takeaway selection, this city centre restaurant has a terrace with a meat-heavy menu. *Patatas bravas* with *jamón* sauce, *jamón croquetas*, plates of *jamón* – you get the picture. Is it a local's hang-out? Not by a long shot. But the views over Plaça de l'Ajuntament are rather handsome.

59 HOMENAJE TABERNA GOURMET

C/ de la Sang 11
Ciutat Vella ②
+34 961 13 33 06
homenaje-gourmet.com

Clad in warm wood and decorated with pictures of pigs snuffling acorns, Homenaje Taberna Gourmet's flagship bar in Canovas is a temple to *jamón*. They have four different types of *jamón ibérico de bellota* alone (made from free range pigs fed on acorns), all artfully sliced by their *maestro cortador*.

60 VIANDAS

C/ de Sant Vicent
Màrtir 14
Ciutat Vella ②
+34 960 62 43 15
viandasstores.com

In a hurry? For *jamón* on the hoof swing by Viandas and grab a cone spilling over with marbled ribbons to take away. Look out for the royal green awnings and windows filled with *bocadillos* stacked like Jenga towers. Nibble a modest 50% Iberian grain-fed *jamón* or go the whole hog with an entire leg of acorn-fed Pata Negra.

The 5 best spots for
LATIN AMERICAN
food

---

61 **LA LLORONA**
C/ del Pintor
Salvador Abril 35
L'Eixample ③
+34 963 28 73 97
taquerialallorona.com

Cheerful service and cool interiors means this taco bar fills up as soon as they open the doors. From jolly groups of mates to polished couples, they're all looking for moreish *cochinita* tacos and *tacos al pastor*. A couple of doors down, sister site Acapulco wine bar is equally jazzy and serves more formal plates.

61 LA LLORONA

62 ASADOR SAN TELMO

C/ de Puerto Rico 14
L'Eixample ③
+34 638 61 18 63
asadorsantelmo.com

The *parrilla* at this Argentinian grill is heaving with sizzling cuts of steak. In the unhurried dining room, couples order the Galician 40-day matured beef to go with intense bottles of Malbec. *Dulce de leche* features in almost every dessert, like the tiramisu with DDL and chocolate cake with DDL mousse.

63 REY TACO

C/ de la Tapineria 9
Ciutat Vella ②
+34 618 66 59 98
reytaco.es

The open kitchen is at the heart of this *taquería*: watch owner Enrique blistering tortillas on the grill like he learned to in his native Mexico. The stools on the street are most popular; folks prop up the bar for a quick grab'n'go. Like it hot? Ask for the spicy sauce kept under the counter.

64 SOL AZTECA

C/ del Pintor
Maella 17
Camins al Grau ⑦
+34 960 88 90 96
restaurantesol
azteca.com

Head to this homely spot, where staff sing along with folk songs on the widescreen telly, for *tamales* cooked in banana leaves and tortillas filled with chicken swimming in a rich mole sauce (there are veggie versions and alternatives). Cool off with a wedge of *tres leches* cake.

65 MANĀW

C/ dels Adreçadors 10
Ciutat Vella ②
+34 960 69 16 32
manaw.es

Manāw's Nikkei Bar serves Asian-Peruvian cuisine, and it's known for punchy flavours, fancy plating and strong cocktails. Ceviche is their speciality; one comes with mussels, prawns and a fiery Peruvian pepper, another with squid *chicharrón*. There's even a ceviche flight for real connoisseurs.

The 5 best
BUDGET-FRIENDLY
restaurants

---

66 **EL TROCITO
DEL MEDIO**
C/ de Blanes 1
Ciutat Vella ②
+34 620 67 78 81

The restaurants around Mercat Central are a mixed bag; avoid the tourist traps and visit this phenomenal local, where a lunch deal *bocadillo*, glass of wine and coffee will set you back 5 euro. Market traders all order from here: spot the famous José and his tray piled high with *cortados* darting back and forth.

67 **CULT CAFÉ**
C/ de l'Arquebisbe
Mayoral 7
Ciutat Vella ②
cultcafe.es

Katarina is the cheery owner of this cafe, which gained a huge loyal following in just over a year. Coffee isn't the cheapest (that's down to the quality beans – Sevilla's Ineffable Coffee) but you can get jazzy avocado toast (dotted with cherry tomatoes and pomegranate molasses) and a *cortado* for a tenner.

68 FELISANO

C/ de Pelai 11
Extramurs ④
+34 963 44 24 23

Popular with a student crowd for its rock-bottom prices, this busy canteen in Chinatown is the best spot for a quick low-budget lunch. Cabinets are chock-a-block with soy-soaked noodles, spring rolls and fried rice. Our tip? Order food that's cooked to order, like pork bao (80 cents) or wonton soup (3 euro).

69 CANTINA MONTEREY

C/ de Baix 46
Ciutat Vella ①
montereydiscos.es

This hippy-rocker bar in El Carmen is an old music-lovers hang-out. It used to sell records, like Peruvian psych or latin funk, but now the only discs they sell are toasted. Tacos are filled with slow-cooked pork, cactus, and chicken in mole sauce, and start from just 2 euro each.

70 RESTAURANTE ALADWAQ

C/ de la Nau 16
Ciutat Vella ②
+34 677 74 42 55
aladwaq.es

There are two affordable Moroccan restaurants on this charming street, but Aladwaq is the cosiest. Order chicken tagine with a hearty broth and finish on a sweet mint tea served on a cute silver tray. Sit outside and spot the wool graffiti embroidered into old buildings nearby.

5 excellent
FINE DINING
restaurants

---

71 EL POBLET

C/ de Correus 8
Ciutat Vella ②
+34 961 11 11 06
elpobletrestaurante.com

Luis Valls heads up this two Michelin-starred quest to make exquisite Valencian food firmly rooted in its surroundings. Plating is theatrical and informative: watch as chefs construct works of art at the table and offer origins of each ingredient. Some plates are poignant: seafood with plastic and sewage emulsion, anyone?

72 RESTAURANTE LIENZO

Plaça de Tetuan 18
Ciutat Vella ②
+34 963 52 10 81
restaurantelienzo.com

Chef and co-owner of Lienzo (canvas in Spanish), María José Martínez is known as the queen of honey, as she uses the ingredient in every dish. She grew up eating honeycomb straight from the beehives in Murcia. On a budget? Their 60-euro lunch menu is a pocket-sized experience.

75 LA SALITA

73 FIERRO

C/ del Doctor
Serrano 4
L'Eixample ③
+34 963 30 52 44
fierrovlc.com

From their dark, edgy restaurant in
the heart of Russafa, chefs Germán
Carrizo y Carito Lourenço cook
imaginative dishes with influences from
their native Argentina. Graze *cremona*,
a star-shaped laminated bread from
Argentina, Galician blue lobster with
green *tomatillo* sauce, and seared wild
duck with the crispiest skin.

74 RICARD CAMARENA RESTAURANT

AT: BOMBAS GENS
CENTRE D'ART
Av. de Burjassot 54
La Saïdia ⑥
+34 963 35 54 18
ricardcamarena.com

With two Michelin stars and a green
star for sustainability, Ricard Camarena
is a local legend. This sleek, wood-
panelled restaurant in a chic art gallery
is the jewel in the restaurant collection.
Dishes are painstakingly researched,
and many of the vegetables are picked
daily at Camarena's kitchen farm, just
eight kilometres away.

75 LA SALITA

C/ de Pere III
el Gran 11
L'Eixample ③
+34 609 33 07 60
*anarkiagroup.com/
inicio/la-salita*

This Michelin-starred restaurant is
relaxed, bohemian, and utterly gorgeous.
Owner and chef Begoña Rodrigo restored
an old family manor house (she couldn't
bear to cover the murals painted by the
old owner's mum; they're hidden behind
false walls in the dining room). Food is
sparky and veg-led.

The 5 finest restaurants in
CHINATOWN

---

76 MEY MEY

C/ de l'Historiador
Diago 19
Extramurs ④
+34 963 82 09 30
mey-mey.com

With its wonderfully kitsch decor (check out the ornamental pond, complete with crane water feature), Mey Mey is one of the oldest Chinese restaurants in Valencia. People have been coming for years for crispy fried *wontons* with little pails of sticky sweet-sour sauce and bamboo steamers filled with dim sum.

77 MIN DOU

C/ de Pelai 31
Extramurs ④
+34 960 06 93 41
restaurantechino
mindou.es

Rows of shiny black chairs, crates of beer stacked in the corner and TV permanently on the news: Min Dou is not a looker, but it's the best spot for authentic Chinese food. There are nearly 200 dishes to choose from, including fried noodles with prawns, chicken feet and gelatinous century eggs.

78 YOUCHA

C/ de Pelai 43
Extramurs ④
+34 666 10 66 68
missudulce.de.
mikecrm.com/sHCThGI

Spangly, futuristic decor surrounds a billion types of bubble tea and a cake cabinet filled with feather-light matcha rolls and milk breads. Choose from Hong Kong-style egg waffles topped with fresh fruit and cream and handmade matcha *mochi*.

79 TIANFUBAZI

C/ de Pelai 54
Extramurs ④
+34 960 06 96 28
tianfubazi.com

This is the place to feast with friends. Beneath red paper lanterns groups huddle around big sunken pots of broth speckled with dried chilli. Plunge hand-pulled noodles, thinly sliced pork and beef tendons into the simmering cauldron. Staff are so informative that even hotpot virgins will feel like seasoned pros after one visit.

80 VI VIET 1

C/ de Pelai 21
Extramurs ④
+34 613 97 06 32
*vivietvalencia.
weebly.com*

New cat on the block Vi Viet 1 made a splash with its neon signage and hip interiors, so much so that they've opened a second branch in L'Eixample. Sit under big wicker lampshades and snack on fried chicken with rice and extra chilli or *pho suon bo*, noodles in an eight-hour beef rib broth.

5 restaurants with
INCREDIBLE
INTERIORS

---

81 TAVELLA

Camí Vell de
Llíria 93
Beniferri ⑤
+34 963 49 87 71
tavellarestaurant.com

Leave the city at the doorstep of this beautiful old manor house, converted into one of the prettiest restaurants in Valencia. Dine in the old kitchen with its original marble worktop, or the sitting room with antique furniture and candy-striped walls. In the kitchen octopus and wild fish is charred over open flame.

83 BEGIN RESTAURANTE

82 VOLTERETA, BIENVENIDO A KIOTO

Passeig de
l'Albereda 51
Camins al Grau ⑦
*voltereta
restaurante.com*

The sushi is not the best in Valencia, but the decor here is undeniably impressive. Choose from two dining rooms: one a take on 16th-century Japan with wood panelling, paper lanterns and creeping vines; the other is a futuristic clash of neon lights and glossy booths.

83 BEGIN RESTAURANTE

C/ de Pascual
i Genís 11
Ciutat Vella ②
beginrestaurante.com

Organic shapes and natural materials set the scene at Begin, a restaurant that wants to transport guests to an imaginary prehistoric era of healthy eating. The cave-like interior is a refuge of veggie-led food. Dive into dishes with cheesy names like 'ancestral hummus' with crudités and 'forest delights' with roasted sweet potato.

84 LA SASTRERÍA

C/ de Josep
Benlliure 42
Poblats Marítims ⑧
+34 960 83 52 25
lasastreriavalencia.com

La Sastreria wants to pay homage to the traditions of Cabanyal, and they started with tiles. There are tiles on tiles on tiles in the maximalist space, just a few paces from the beachfront. Food is sea-led, with dishes like oysters on ice, shrimp *croquetas* and grilled razor clams.

85 CAFÉ DE LAS HORAS

C/ del Comte
d'Almodóvar 1
Ciutat Vella ①
+34 963 91 73 36
cafedelashoras.com

More is more at Las Horas, a mad mash-up of a regal British tea house and a burlesque nightclub. Beneath glittering chandeliers, every inch is covered in antique paintings, velvet drapes and bouquets of roses. An eccentric crowd is there to get tipsy on *Agua de Valencia* and tap their toes to live bossa nova.

5 places for a
SUGAR HIT

---

86 MÒLT

C/ de Burriana 14
L'Eixample ③
+34 634 49 39 46
moltdepa.es

Sourdough bread with a crackly crust is the star of the show (it's the best in Valencia), but don't overlook the cakes. Sniff out the neon orange sign, it's just a 10-minute detour from the well-trodden shops of Carrer de Colón, and discover a counter decorated with Swedish cardamom buns and buttery almond financiers.

87 SUKAR

C/ de la Pau 16
Ciutat Vella ②
+34 960 81 28 73

Go hungry to Sukar; everything on the counter is delightful. Croissants get a glamorous makeover with hazelnut praline and Valrhona white chocolate, or mascarpone cream with coffee and amaretto. Go early for the cruffins: fun flavours like peanut butter and salted caramel sell out in a flash.

88 PASSAGE À PARIS

C/ del Doctor
Sumsi 29
L'Eixample ③
+34 658 51 84 71
passageaparis.es

Like the *pâtisseries* of Montmartre, Passage à Paris stops passers-by in their tracks with its gold lettering, exquisitely decorated cakes and the aroma of buttery croissants. Co-owners Nelly and Fabien left Paris to bring feather-light *religieuse au chocolat* and proper *tarte citron* to Valencia.

89 HORNO Y PASTELERÍA ALFONSO MARTÍNEZ

C/ d'Ercilla 17
Ciutat Vella ②
+34 963 91 60 79
*horno-y-pasteleria-
alfonso-martinez.
negocio.site*

One of the oldest bakeries in Valencia, the family-owned Horno y Pastelería Alfonso Martínez makes traditional cakes, some of which haven't changed since they opened their doors in 1886. They specialise in *panquemado*, *coca* cake with raisins and nuts, roasted pumpkin cake, and aniseed rolls.

90 MOCHISAN

C/ de Martí l'Humà 4
Extramurs ④
+34 625 06 56 13
mochi-san.com

Andrea Valls left her cello studies to open this adorable Japanese *mochi* cafe, an idea that she came up with during lockdown. Inside she makes the squidgy, chewy rice balls fresh – no frozen shortcuts here – and fills them with matcha cream or *Agua de Valencia* with orange mousse and a cava core.

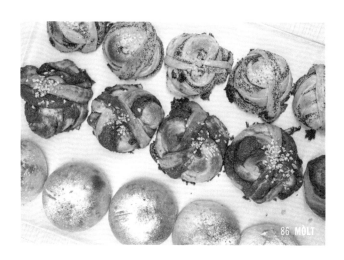

86 MÒLT

The 5 best places to eat
CHEESECAKE

---

91 CANALLA BISTRO
C/ del Mestre Josep
Serrano 5
L'Eixample ③
+34 963 74 05 09
canallabistro.com

Cheesecake is one of the many things that Valencia does brilliantly. Golden on the outside, gooey in the middle and properly cheesy. At Canalla Bistro, Ricard Camarena serves a top-notch slice which holds its shape (just). Tip: buy Camarena's cheesecake to take away from Solaz in Mercat Central.

93 JULIET

92 LLISA NEGRA

C/ de Pascual
i Genís 10
Ciutat Vella ②
+34 963 94 60 79
llisanegra.com

This fancy spot by Quique Dacosta is better known for its glitzy decor and paella cooked over open fire, but their fondant cheesecake, with a liquid centre that pools in the plate, deserves its time in the spotlight. Keep an eye out for the chocolate version, which occasionally graces the menu.

93 JULIET

C/ de Bonaire 22
Ciutat Vella ②
+34 680 96 31 71

Owner Julia left her job in biotechnology to follow her dream of opening a bakery. Barely cooked cinnamon rolls are the best in the city and cookies with blow torched marshmallows and liquid fillings are insane, but chocolate cheesecake dotted with rose petals is the one that people fall head-over-heels for.

94 VERMÚDEZ

Gran Via de les
Germanies 21
L'Eixample ③
+34 963 03 47 74
vermudez.es

Based on the edge of Russafa with a classy fit out, Vermúdez is the spot to *vermutear*, but it also serves a heavenly slice. Chocolate cheesecake is part liquid, part ambrosia from the Gods, and comes served with silky vanilla ice cream.

95 BAR CREMAET

Av. del Port 20
El Pla del Real ⑥
+34 960 83 52 21
barcremaet.com

Bar Cremaet is part of Gastroadictos, a small restaurant group that takes local classics and polishes them up a bit. Decor here is modern with a smattering of nostalgia, there are retro typefaces and a long stainless-steel bar. The cheesecake is divine: light, creamy, and best enjoyed on the sunny terrace.

5 awesome
ICE-CREAM
parlours

---

96 VÉNETA

Passeig de Neptú 14
Poblats Maritims ⑧
heladosveneta.com

No wonder there are queues here, Véneta was named third best parlour in the world in 2020. Find three sites: Plaça de la Reina, Carrer de Ribera and a more glam beach-front shop with lots of air-conditioned seating. *Galleta de la abuela* is biscuity, buttery, and was named best ice cream in Spain.

97 LA PECERA

C/ de Ribera 3
Ciutat Vella ②
+34 693 23 57 86
wearelapecera.es

Spot this cool Madrid-based chain a mile off with its Las Vegas neon lights of Spongebob Squarepants and Pacman. Inside they serve ice cream in *taiyakis*, a Japanese-style fish-shaped cone. Choose your flavour and add fun toppings like sprinkles, mini oreos and chocolate sauce.

98 VALENTINO GELATO

C/ d'En Sanç 13
Ciutat Vella ②
+34 656 70 48 30
valentinogelato.es

From the outside this looks like just another run-of-the-mill *heladería*, but the focus here is squarely on the *gelato*. There are the usual suspects, like Kinder and *dulce de leche*, but what sets them apart is their vegan range: watermelon, blueberry and a surprisingly creamy chocolate.

99 LLINARES

Plaça de la Reina 6
Ciutat Vella ②
+34 963 91 74 66
heladeriasllinares.com

With its roots in the 1930s, this family-run joint has a rich history but with wacky flavours like tortilla, gazpacho and gin they're certainly not old-fashioned. Join the crowds at their Willy Wonka takeaway and grab a cone of *Turrón de Jijona*, made with nougat and toasted almonds.

100 LUCCIANO'S

Plaça de
l'Ajuntament 2
Ciutat Vella ②
luccianos.net

A ceiling-height toy soldier and a hot-air balloon welcome visitors at this superb parlour, where kids faceplant tubs of strawberry *gelato* in the carriage of a life-sized train. It's like tumbling into a toy box – with ice cream. Don't miss the fountain of milk chocolate which they drizzle over cones.

5 LOCAL DELICACIES
that are full of history

---

101 ESGARRAET

Esgarrar means 'tear' in Valencian, and cooks have been tearing cod for *esgarraet* since time immemorial. It's made with *bacalao*, sweet roasted red pepper, garlic and oodles of olive oil. Some believe the dish originated in Cabanyal, although others think that it is city-wide, as it beautifully combines the farmland and the sea.

102 ALL I PEBRE

In the canals of the Albufera, wild eels swim between the reeds. They're the main ingredient of this stew made with garlic, peppers and tomato first whipped up by fishermen on the shores of the lake. It is a rare gem in the city centre (La Salita serves a version with white pepper and lemon rind).

103 CLOTXINA

Mussels? Nearly. This is *clotxina*: Valencia's smaller, more delicate variety. Grown near the port, the farming practise dates back to the 19th century and it is a trade that's passed down through generations. Find the seasonal delicacy on most menus from late April to August.

104 BUÑUELOS

A popular treat sold on street corners during Fallas, *buñuelos* may have been brought to Spain by the Moors from North Africa. In the 16th century the Morisco population ate fried dough balls drizzled in honey. The 18th century saw *buñuelos* mixed with pumpkin being sold at the early Fallas bonfires.

105 TURRÓN

This nougat bar is a Christmas stalwart, but its origins stretch way back. Some historians point to the ancient Greeks, who prepared honey and nuts for Olympic athletes. The first record of *turrón* was by an Arab doctor in the 11th century, and by the 15th century it was hugely popular, especially in Alicante.

104 BUÑUELOS

70 PLACES
FOR A DRINK

The 5 best cafes for a
CAFFEINE FIX

---

106 NEWS & COFFEE
Plaça del Doctor Collado
Ciutat Vella ②
+34 659 47 90 47
newsandcoffee.eu

News & Coffee is the Barcelona-based group that revive Spain's historic newspaper kiosks with a hot new magazine selection and excellent coffee. Flick through the interior eye-candy of *Openhouse* and the fresh fashion in *Pop* while sipping a coffee on the bonny bench (co-owner Albert made it himself).

107 FAV COFFEE
C/ del Cronista Carreres 1
Ciutat Vella ②

Sergio and Ksenia moved to Valencia from Madrid and brought the capital's stellar coffee scene to this converted old pharmacy. Find the usual suspects like perfect flat whites and oat milk lattes alongside cooler options for scorching days like matcha iced lattes and kale kombucha.

108 FRAN CAFE

C/ de Puerto Rico 29
L'Eixample ③
+34 610 12 11 55

Fran is the name of an imaginary customer that owner Vicky dreamt up: she drinks flat whites, hangs out in Russafa and buys cool secondhand clothes. Sound familiar? Go for the coffee and nibble *alfajores* on the terracotta banquette where Devil's Ivy with heart-shaped leaves hang like bunting.

109 TALLAT

C/ de la Barraca 25
Poblats Marítims ⑧
+34 960 83 64 46
tallatcoffee.com

Tallat pops against historic houses with minimalism and woodchip counter, but in a nod to its heritage the shopfront sign mimics the original 1951 design. They're busy bees: not only do they roast their own coffee, they run tons of tasting events and whip up a mean orange cake, too.

110 RETROGUSTO COFFEEMATES

AT: MERCAT CENTRAL
DE VALÈNCIA,
PUESTOS 169-170
Plaça de la Ciutat
de Bruges
Ciutat Vella ②
+34 637 95 92 70
*retrogusto
coffeemates.com*

Shopping at Mercat Central? Make a pit stop at Retrogusto. Don't be fooled by its size; the owner of Michelin-starred restaurant Riff says it's the best in Valencia. Founder Martina must have memorised hundreds of orders: regulars prop up the bar, ask for the 'usual' and set the world to rights.

5 places to drink
HORCHATA

---

111 **HORCHATERÍA DE SANTA CATALINA**
Plaça de Santa Caterina 6
Ciutat Vella ②
+34 963 91 23 79
horchateria santacatalina.com

Horchata is made from chufa, the root of yellow nutsedge. It's soaked, blended and sieved and hey presto: *horchata*. Some like it chilled, others icy like a slushy (*granizado*). Fancy a glass? Horchatería de Santa Catalina has over 200 years of experience – it's worth going to see the gorgeous tiles alone.

112 VACHATA

**C/ de Mossèn
Femenia 22
L'Eixample ③
+34 640 17 53 42
*vachatahorchata.com***

Horchata runs in the veins of Marta Planells, the granddaughter of some of Valencia's leading chufa producers and vendors. She's taken the concept and scrubbed it up for Russafa's style-savvy crowd, with sunshine yellow tiles and shiny bar stools like a 1950s diner.

113 HORCHATERÍA EL COLLADO

**C/ d'Ercilla 13
Ciutat Vella ②
+34 963 91 62 77**

This classic *horchatería* has been pouring frosty glasses since 1892, and the decor has barely changed. Staff in hairnets and pinafores serve big tables of families crowded and chattering around plastic trays of *fartons*. Don't miss the black and white photos of the owners and their family dotted around.

114 LA HUERTANA

AT: MERCAT CENTRAL DE VALÈNCIA, PUESTOS 148-152
**Plaça de la Ciutat
de Bruges
Ciutat Vella ②
+34 963 82 91 28**

The long marble bar of this stall in Mercat Central is heaven for *horchata* fans. Sweltering? Order *mitad y mitad*, half frozen half liquid *horchata* for a crisp, ice-cold cup. It is an acquired taste, so La Huertana serves freshly squeezed orange juice and fruit smoothies if you don't love it – yet.

115 HORCHATERÍA DANIEL

AT: MERCAT DE COLÓN
**C/ de Jorge Juan 19
L'Eixample ③
+34 961 85 88 66
*horchateria-daniel.es***

Third generation owner Daniel Tortajada still remembers the day Salvador Dalí's Rolls Royce pulled up to try their *horchata*. The photo of Dalí is proudly displayed in his newest cafe on Carrer del Mar, but the spot in Mercat de Colón, with its swooping ceilings and sun-dappled terrace, is the best.

5 places that serve the perfect
CREMAET

---

116 BAR RESTAURANTE ROJAS CLEMENTE

Plaça de Rojas
Clemente
Extramurs ④
+34 963 91 71 97
bar-restaurante-rojas-
clemente.eatbu.com

Almuerzo usually ends on a *cremaet*: a liqueur coffee made with rum, sugar, lemon and cinnamon. The ingredients are set alight before an espresso is pulled over the top. Fancy one? Start with Bar Restaurante Rojas Clemente. The barista makes lemony *cremaets* with a whisper of alcohol.

117 LA CHATA ULTRAMARINOS

C/ del Literat
Azorín 4
L'Eixample ③
+34 675 66 00 17
lachata
ultramarinos.com

Cremaet is nice, but *cremaet* XXL is nicer. Find it at the Russafa branch of La Chata, a small group of delis stocked with goodies like Cantabrian *boquerones* and local organic wine. At their deli-bar on Literat Azorín the *cremaet* requires twice as much rum as usual (around four shots), ice cream and a chocolate cookie on top.

118 RESTAURANTE ESPINOSA

C/ d'Espinosa 18-20
Extramurs ④
+34 963 92 30 57

This polished, popular restaurant is run by the second generation of the Carrilero family, considered *almuerzo* kingpins. Ingredients bought that morning fill the counter. Whatever your *bocadillo* choice, don't miss out on a crisp, clean *cremaet*, topped with silky *crema* and coffee beans.

119 LA CANTINA

C/ del Literat
Azorín 13-A
L'Eixample ③
+34 653 94 40 26
lacantinaderuzafa.
wixsite.com

Hidden from street view, La Cantina looks at traditional cuisine from a modern perspective. People come for the affordable *almuerzos* overlooking the lush allotment where they grow beans, pumpkins and lemons. The *chivito* with runny eggs and stewed beef is a must. Finish with a round of perfectly prepared *cremaets*.

120 BAR CONGO

Av. del Regne
de València 51
L'Eixample ③
+34 960 81 52 82
barcongovalencia.com

Óscar Casasnovas and Pepa Gil have sprinkled their hospitality magic on this historic bar, scrubbing it up without losing its character. On the terrace old fellas drink beers in wooden safari chairs, while indoors red leather banquette seats lend a 1950s feel. *Cremaets* are made unhurriedly, and to a tee.

119 LA CANTINA

5 bars with a
FASCINATING
HISTORY

---

121 CAFÉ MADRID
C/ de l'Abadia
de Sant Martí 10
Ciutat Vella ②
+34 960 66 05 07
myrhotels.com/
restauracion/
cafe-madrid

In the 20th century, the writers and intellectuals at Café Madrid were getting bored of fizz; they wanted something new. In 1956 owner Constant Gil invented *Agua de Valencia* (cava, gin, vodka, sugar and orange juice), and it became their drink of choice. To this day the cocktail and the bar is still going strong.

122 ALMA DEL TEMPLE
AT: CARO HOTEL
C/ de l'Almirall 14
Ciutat Vella ①
+34 963 15 52 87
almadeltemple.com

Owners of the five-star Caro Hotel had no idea what was lurking in the basement when they bought it. The Gothic palace stands on the old walls of Valencia, marked by the remains of a 12th-century Moorish wall. The restaurant is now split in two by the beautifully preserved relic.

123 CHRISTOPHER
C/ de Pinzón 17
Ciutat Vella ①
+34 664 42 22 02
christopher
cocteles.com

This retro, movie-themed joint opened in 1971. Together with a handful of fellow indies, Christopher (there's a pic of Christopher Lee by the stairs) brought bohemian interests like film and music to what was then an up-and-coming El Carmen, blooming with radical thinkers after the dictatorship had come to an end.

124 CASA GUILLERMO

C/ del Progrés 15
Poblats Maritims ⑧
+34 963 67 91 77
casaguillermo1957.com

Fancy rubbing shoulders with royalty...? Anchovy royalty that is. Founded in 1957, Casa Guillermo was home to the king and queen of anchovies, they sold the best in the city. Now their daughter Amparo carries on their legacy. She buys, cleans and prepares the anchovies by hand, just like her parents before her.

125 CAFÉ SANT JAUME

C/ dels Cavallers 51
Ciutat Vella ①
+34 963 91 24 01
cafesantjaume.com

This exquisite bar has been serving drinks in El Carmen for over 30 years, but its history goes back further. A former apothecary, it was the first pharmacy opened by Cañizares Domingo in 1899. He helped invent ointments and medicines, and improved health and living standards in the area.

125 CAFÉ SANT JAUME

The 5 best
ROOFTOPS and TERRACES

---

126 **LA TERRAZA DE BLANQ**
AT: BLANQ CARMEN HOTEL
C/ de la Blanqueria 11
Ciutat Vella ①
+34 962 05 77 00
blanqhotels.com/
carmen

This hotel rooftop comes to life when the heat of the day has cooled off. Tables of friends order playful cocktails or chilled *albariño* while they watch the sun set and the Torres dels Serrans light up. Arrive early to bagsy the swinging rattan chair. The pool is just for hotel guests, sadly.

127 **ÀTIC**
AT: PALAU ALAMEDA
C/ de Muñoz Seca 2
El Pla del Real ⑥
+34 963 54 51 76
palaualameda.com

This multi-venue space is famous for its *tardeos* (early parties starting from around 5 pm). On the top floor is Àtic, a large terrace with views over the Jardí del Túria. The day-to-night hang-out is a good spot to share a bottle of *verdejo*, and they pump up the music with floor-fillers after dark.

128 LA PLAÇA GASTRO MERCAT

AT: EL CORTE INGLÉS
C/ de Colón 25
Ciutat Vella ②
+34 961 81 87 00
elcorteingles.es

This giant department store has a secret on its top floor. Bypass the ironing boards and garden furniture to find a sixth-floor canteen with gorgeous views of the city. OK, the restaurant is a little drab, but the terrace is usually deserted. It's a low-profile spot with excellent local wine and jamón. Perfect for avoiding crowds.

129 LA PERFUMERÍA

AT: HOTEL PALACIO VALLIER
Plaça de Manises 7
Ciutat Vella ①
+34 960 66 13 07
myrhotels.com

A 20-euro minimum spend deters many, which means that couples on date nights get the chic rooftop of this five-star hotel to themselves. It's overlooked only by the Gothic tower of Palau de la Generalitat, and it has the best views over Plaça de la Mare de Déu. Exquisite cocktails are served from 5 pm.

130 MADRE

C/ d'Eugènia Viñes 227
Poblats Maritims ⑧
+34 626 28 73 53
lawebdemadre.com

Cumbia music plays out over the avocado-green terrace of Madre, a lively pad that serves cracking cocktails and food with a heavy South American lean. Expect spicy ceviche made with ají amarillo, vegan nachos and tacos al pastor. Finish on a coffee made with Bluebell's locally roasted beans.

5 hot BEACH BARS
and CHIRINGUITOS

---

131 **LA MÁS BONITA CHIRINGUITO**
AT: PLATJA DE LA PATACONA
**Opposite Passeig
Marítim de la
Patacona 11
Alboraia** ⑧
+34 961 14 36 11
*lamasbonita.es/en/
restaurants/chiringuito*

If the queues for La Más Bonita's restaurant are too much, walk to their sister site in the sand. Follow the wooden walkway to find the boho shack (*chiringuito* in Castellano) with 360-degree beach views, salad bowls, healthy smoothies and strong cocktails. Open from May to October.

132 CHIRINGO

AT: PLATJA DE LA PATACONA
**Opposite residencia
Ballesol
Passeig Marítim de
la Patacona 83
Alboraia** ⑧
+34 663 28 79 48

This *chiringuito* on the golden stretch of Patacona is a lively number. In the afternoon it's the best base to listen to the waves falling against the sand with a *tinto de verano*. There are tables that can be reserved, sandwiches in kitchen, and funky dance on the speakers. It all goes well with sun-kissed shoulders and a potent *mojito*.

133 LA GIRAFE

**Av. Mare Nostrum 10
Alboraia** ⑧
+34 963 68 44 12
lagirafe.es

After a dip in the deep blue, make sandy tracks to Patacona for a jug of sangría in the shaded terrace of La Girafe. The food isn't the best on this row of restaurants, but their quirky decor (the vintage bus-turned-kitchen wows kids and adults alike) makes for a chilled place to refuel.

134 CHIRINGUITO TRES14 BEACH

AT: PLATJA DE LA PATACONA
Alboraia ⑧
+34 601 63 36 96

Savvy locals head to the last *chiringuito* on Patacona beach for the best sundowners. It's a walk but it's worth the trip to this solar-powered shack. Here, a happy crowd dance in the sand with piña coladas to a lively roster of DJs and local sound systems. Even Sunday evenings are packed.

135 MEDI SURF CAFÉ

**Av. Mare Nostrum 7
Alboraia** ⑧
+34 644 55 28 31
*mediterraneansurf.com/
puzol/#casa-mar*

It's a couple of streets back from the sea, but the beach vibes are strong with this one. Part of a small collection of surf schools, Medi Surf Café is where beach bums come to graze on poke bowls of salmon, avocado and *wakame* or ripped burgers with guacamole and cheese.

5 SUNNY SQUARES

for a cold caña

---

136 PLAÇA DEL COL·LEGI DEL PATRIARCA
Ciutat Vella ②

Who doesn't love sitting in a sleepy, sun-drenched square with a frosty beer? The bars in this *plaça* face the historic home of Valencia University, a pretty building that dates back to the 15th century. Take a seat under the shade of an orange tree while children play next to the bronze and marble fountain.

137 PLAÇA DE LA REINA
Ciutat Vella ②

This new square was pedestrianised, scrubbed up, and kitted out with a cooling misty jungle to put it back at the heart of Valencia's old town. Pull up a chair at L'Abadia for a cold *caña* next to the cathedral, which turns peachy-pink in the late afternoon sun.

138 PLAÇA DE LOPE DE VEGA
Ciutat Vella ②

This small square is a good spot to watch the world go by. Formerly known as Plaça de Yerbas, it used to be a market hub where traders sold vegetables from their farms. Now, the square is best known for being home to the church of Santa Catalina, which dates back to 1238.

139 PLAÇA DE LA MARE DE DÉU
Ciutat Vella ①

If historical monuments, Roman roots and people watching is your thing, count on Plaça de la Mare de Déu (Plaza de la Virgen in Castellano) to deliver. The *plaça's* basilica – a baroque beauty, sweetly scented with incense and completed in 1667 – is the best eye-candy.

140 PLAÇA DE CÁNOVAS
L'Eixample ③

This *plaça* is dominated by a gargantuan example of Valencian Modernism, Edifici Xapa. The 200-metre-long façade is best admired from across the street in El Timbre, a traditional bar with a handful of terrace tables that are popular with an after-work crowd.

139 PLAÇA DE LA MARE DE DÉU

5 top bars for
V E R M O U T H *fans*

---

141 **TABERNA
LA SAMORRA**
C/ de l'Almodí 14
Ciutat Vella ①
+34 640 73 51 00
tabernalasamorra.com

This lovely restaurant in the old town is so good it could have featured in dozens of these lists. Take a wooden stool at the beautifully tiled bar, where spirits are stacked up to the ceiling. Pair vermouth with anchovies or smoked sardines, and come back later to pick at brilliant *figatells*.

142 **BOCATÍN**
C/ de Calatrava 21
Ciutat Vella ①
+34 963 92 51 16

Hunkered in the tangled streets of El Carmen, look for the baby blue shutters of this timeless *vermutería*. Beneath the archways regulars sip on tumblers of well-balanced Xaloneret made with muscatel grapes and graze on fried aubergines drizzled with honey.

143 AQUARIUM

Gran Via del
Marqués del Túria 57
L'Eixample ③
+34 963 51 00 40

The faded, ritzy glamour of this nautical-themed tavern is a delight. Glossy dark wood cladding, portholes, and racing green leather benches all date back to around 1957 (although staff reckon it could be older). Waiters in white suits and shiny gold buttons deliver impeccable vermouths and even better martinis.

144 BENVOLGUT

AT: MERCAT CENTRAL DE
VALÈNCIA, PUESTOS 153-159
Plaça de la Ciutat
de Bruges
Ciutat Vella ②
+34 605 96 59 98
benvolgut.es

Vermouth on tap is the dream and Miguel, owner of Benvolgut, is living it. Enjoy a glass of *vermut de grifo* with olives and a wedge of lemon at his stall in Mercat Central, where he cheerily chats to customers about his range of locally made beers, snacks and gin with brilliant retro branding.

145 TABERNA LA SÉNIA

C/ de la Sénia, 2
Ciutat Vella ②
+34 611 49 76 77
tabernalasenia.es

Central yet secluded, this tiny *taberna* transformed into a popular spot after it was featured in the Michelin Guide a few years ago. There are three vermouths on offer: red, white and an artisan vermouth from Teulada. Pair with *boquerones* marinated in vermouth and Valencian oranges or olives in extra virgin olive oil.

5 ROMANTIC BARS
to fall in love with

146 **ANGOLO DIVINO**
C/ de l'Almirall
Cadarso 14
L'Eixample ③
+34 667 76 48 96
angolo-divino-wine-
bar.negocio.site

In this cutesy wine bar in La Gran Via, couples order creamy *burratas* and big sharing boards of salamis to go with their bottles. The wine is exclusively from Italy: there are dry sparkling reds from Modena and a punchy pinot noir by winemaking heavyweight Klaus Lentsch.

147 **GRAN MARTÍNEZ**
Av. del Port 318
Poblats Maritims ⑧
+34 963 85 06 65
granmartinez.com

The atmosphere is electric at Gran Martínez, a sultry bar in Cabanyal that turned heads when it launched. Owners incorporated lots of the old pharmacy's woodwork: they even put the turntables on antique cabinets. Listen to obscure Egyptian disco and sip a lip-puckering Fuego Manzana.

148 TERRA À VINS

C/ de Ciscar 48
L'Eixample ③
+34 960 08 18 55
terraavins.com

With its rustic decor, rare and interesting wines and cosy tables for two, Terra à Vins is one of the best wine dens in La Gran Via. Ask the bartender (and wine encyclopaedia) Pablo what he's pouring today, maybe a fine champagne by Domaine Dehours or perhaps a Palo Cortado sherry.

149 OSTERIA

C/ dels Tomasos 20
L'Eixample ③
+34 962 06 61 72

At night this *trattoría* is magical; its small tables lit by candles in wine bottles laden with so much dripping wax they look like they've been painted by Dalí. Loved-up diners order wine by the bottle and nibble on Tuscan salami and cheese from Lombardy. Save room for dessert: a wedge of ricotta and fruit tart.

150 BODEGA ALBARIZAS

C/ d'Antoni Suárez 29
El Pla del Real ⑥
+34 960 17 75 25
bodegaalbarizas.
eatbu.com

A play on owner Alba's name, the matchbox-sized Bodega Albarizas is a trove of wine, some of which she makes with help from friends in nearby bodegas. Peep through the circular wooden door to see friends toasting with big glasses of rioja over wooden boards of *jamón*.

The 5 coolest
CRAFT BEER *bars*

---

151 TYRIS ON TAP
C/ de la Taula de
Canvis 6
Ciutat Vella ①
+34 961 13 28 73
cervezatyris.com

Close to Mercat Central, the terrace tables of this brewery-owned pub are filled with an indie, international crowd. They sip Tyris' Bavarian-style lager and 6% IPAs against the backdrop of crumbling buildings and politically charged graffiti (it's by Elias Taño, and quotes Valencian poet Vicent Andrés Estellés).

152 STONECASTLE BREWERY
C/ de l'Arquitecte
Alfaro 8
Poblats Maritims ⑧
+34 963 81 04 07

Maurice learnt how to brew traditional American ales in Portland, before he moved to Valencia to set up his own brew tap. Find him pouring pints in an old car workshop, which he meticulously refurbished with vintage motorbikes and custom wrought iron.

153 ZERO 11
C/ de Pere III
el Gran 15
L'Eixample ③

As well as a big line up of local beer heroes – like hazy IPAs by Sáez & Son – Zero 11 has a jolly events calendar with everything from artisan markets to live music. They have three sites but Cabanyal is the coolest; its cavernous polished concrete walls are plastered with stickers and wacky graffiti.

154 **OLHÖPS**

C/ de Sueca 21
L'Eixample ③
+34 611 75 29 40
olhops.com

Like something straight out of Copenhagen, Olhöps is all plywood seating and exposed pipework. Nine taps pour modern brews from around the world, and the fridges are packed with over 100 different colourful tins. The spontaneously-fermented beetroot beer by Barcelona's Cyclic Beer Farm is utterly wild.

155 **THE MARKET CRAFT BEER**

C/ de les Danses 5
Ciutat Vella ①
+34 644 33 31 27

Fans of British pub culture will love The Market, a boozer with walnut-stained wood and carved archways that feel cosy and a tad punky. Punters come in squinting from the sunny street to find a cool, dark booth and drink hazy DIPAs by Basqueland, or tins of raspberry jam chocolate doughnut by Andalucia's Malandar.

154 OLHÖPS

5 modern
NATURAL WINE *bars*

---

156 LOS PICOS
Plaça de Manuel
Granero 20
L'Eixample ③

Why isn't Los Picos, one of Valencia's best coffee bars, in the coffee section? Because it's also a pretty sweet spot to sip natural wine. Owners are batty about the stuff, and pour glasses of chilled juicy French reds on the mellow, sun-dappled terrace.

157 BLISS
C/ de la Reina
Na Maria 1
L'Eixample ③
+34 611 34 90 08

Devised by Sophie and Matías from France and Argentina respectively, Bliss is an unstuffy home to low-intervention wines. Early birds nibble on coffee and croissants and in the evening they bring out the big guns: toasty Cabernets from Alicante and well-balanced whites by fourth-generation winemaker Samuel Cano.

158 MEVINO
C/ de Josep
Benlliure 117
Poblats Maritims ⑧
+34 961 05 74 98
mevino.es

From fizzy orange bottles by local heroes Bodegas Cueva to young malbecs by French biodynamic icon Fabien Jouves, Mevino has natural and low-intervention wine down. Their USP? Excellent tapas. Order artichoke with parmesan and black olives or a hoofing great cheese board with focaccia like bubblewrap.

159 L'ALQUIMISTA

C/ de Lluís de
Santàngel 1
L'Eixample ③
+34 685 20 14 13

Mario Tarroni has built a loyal fanbase for his handmade pasta, but his wine list deserves time in the spotlight. They have been championing natural winemakers since before it was a thing. A changing menu might feature silky chardonnays by Jean François Ryon or dry orange wines from Serbia.

160 VIVEVINO

C/ del Músic
Padilla 2
L'Eixample ③
+34 960 22 81 57

Natty wine newbie? Don't fret – Martha and Nieves will skilfully deduct your perfect glass in record time. Go funky or classic, there's room for both in this cobalt-blue wine bar in Russafa. Try perky biodynamic bottles from Solo el Amor Salvara el el Mundo and hippy moscatels by Bodegas Cueva.

5 *tiny* **TABERNAS**
that are totally charming

---

161 TASCA SOROLLA
C/ dels Drets 27
Ciutat Vella ②
+34 601 25 52 90
tascasorolla.com

The handful of stools at this intriguing *tasca* fill up in seconds. Owner Ximo mans both the bar and the kitchen, dishing out cold beer and high-quality seasonal tapas to his regulars. The changing menu might feature grilled octopus, briney sardines and charred marbled steak.

162 BALTASAR SEGUÍ
C/ d'Emili Baró 17
Benimaclet ⑥
+34 963 69 13 84

Floor to ceiling barrels, all groaning with local wine, line the entrance of this low-fi bodega in Benimaclet. Bring your own flagon and fill it with white (1,60 euro a litre) or red (1,80 a litre). The wine shop at the back has tables cooled by plug-in room fans, where locals get merry and sip pink cava.

163 TASCA ANGEL
C/ de la Puríssima 1
Ciutat Vella ②
+34 963 91 78 35

Sardinitas de la casa are the speciality at Tasca Angel, and people pack in like, err, sardines to try them. The fish are carefully filleted and grilled, then finished with a dash of olive oil, chopped garlic and parsley. Stand elbow-to-elbow with fellow diners and sip a burly barrel-aged rioja.

164 BAR CHÉ TABERNA VASCA

Av. del Regne
de València 9
L'Eixample ③
+34 963 74 65 25

This *taberna* is nearly 100 years old and most things haven't moved an inch. It boasts a traditional line-up of tapas, like squid in its own ink and snails. The original cash machine with *pesetas* and *centimos* still stands to attention, and the dining room booths are dressed with green gingham tablecloths.

165 OLIVÍ

C/ de Calatrava 4
Ciutat Vella ①

Raquel and Ezequiel have an exquisite eye. They saved the antique shelves of an old shop, added art deco stained glass, and put up vintage wallpaper. Throw in some excellent wine and friendly service, and the result is a lovable bar that everyone wishes was their local.

5 bars with
BEAUTIFUL VIEWS

---

166 VILLA INDIANO
Cami de l'Estació 4
Burjassot
+34 621 34 17 51
villaindiano.com

A 100-year-old palace was transformed into this trendy spot, with an enormous garden where children play in sandpits while parents graze on tacos and beer and admire the sweeping views over *la huerta*. Villa Indiano is just 20 minutes by tram, but it feels a million miles away from the city centre.

167 TERRAZA MALABAR
AT: VELES E VENTS
C/ Marina Real
Juan Carlos I
Poblats Maritims ⑧
+34 652 10 25 18
veleseventsvalencia.es

DJs, VIP tables and bottles of Belvedere on ice isn't everyone's jam, but the views from this wraparound balcony in the iconic Veles e Vents building will be universally appreciated. Claim a sofa and strap in for a buzzy, boisterous night with views of sailboats and the twinkling port.

168 ATENEA SKY
C/ de Moratín 12
Ciutat Vella ②
+34 661 02 54 59
ateneasky.com

Take the lift to the eighth floor of this office block to find a polished cocktail bar with breathtaking views. With your drink purchase you gain access to the terrace above the bar, where a secluded swing chair with 360-degree views over the rooftops is absolutely begging for romantic proposals.

169 LISBOA RESTOBAR

**Plaça del Doctor
Collado 9
Ciutat Vella** ②
+34 963 91 94 84
lisboarestobar.com

Take a seat under the 100-year-old olive tree outside Lisboa Restobar for something more down to earth. Cocktails are their speciality, and the *Agua de Valencia* is especially popular. The best views are on Sundays, when Lindy Hop rock up and the *plaça* fills with energetic, joyful dancing.

170 SKY BAR

AT: SEA YOU HOTEL
**Plaça del Tribunal
de les Aigües 5
Poblats Marítims** ⑧
+34 963 21 43 30
*seayouhotel.es/en/
sky-bar.html*

The hotel is a bit naff (stag dos seem to love it here) and the drinks aren't cheap, but it's still a treat to visit the top floor of Sea You Hotel. It's a testament to the views, which stretch from the sea, over the patchwork of pastel-coloured buildings, to the mountains.

167 TERRAZA MALABAR

5 places to start a
FUN NIGHT OUT

---

171 THE BASEMENT SOUNDSYSTEM
thebasementxxx.com

These house music dealers pop up at venues around the city with their own brand of cool, no-nonsense events designed to get the crowd off their phones and on the dancefloor. Expect clubnights in Ciutat de les Arts i les Ciències and 12-hour non-stop parties in a *finca* surrounded by orange groves.

172 PETER ROCK CLUB
C/ de Quart 26
Ciutat Vella ①
peterrockclub.es

A timeless, live-music venue with a good crowd, Peter Rock is known as *la casa del rock*. Inside, the drum kit is plastered with stickers and quotes on the wall from AC/DC, among others. From Santana cover bands to Argentinian rock and local heavy metal there's an eclectic line-up to choose from.

173 16 TONELADAS

C/ de Ricardo Micó 3
Campanar ⑤
+34 963 49 45 84
16toneladas.com

Want to get deeper into the local music scene? Across the Túria, 16 Toneladas is rooted in 1950s rock and roll, but plays everything from 1970s funk and modern punk. They're big fans of vinyl too; keep an eye out for disco nights, like the funk and soul parties with local DJs.

174 RADIO CITY

C/ de Santa Teresa 19
Ciutat Vella ②
+34 963 91 41 51
radiocityvalencia.es

Open since 1979, Radio City has always attracted artists, music heads, misfits, and folks looking to boogie. The space is split in two: one side is a pub where punters chatter over a beer, and the other is a compact club where bands and DJs play 'till the small hours.

175 SPLENDINI BAR I DISCOS

C/ de Sogorb 10
L'Eixample ③
+34 679 61 18 96
*splendinibaridiscos.
company.site*

DJs dance in between queuing offbeat funk and soul tracks at this record shop-meets-bar, while a chilled crowd make friends on the communal table. Like their vibe? Owners often play sets at clubs. Look out for Splendini on the line-up at places like Oven Club and Radio City.

BANGARANG

5 cool
ECO-FRIENDLY *shops*

181 HINOJO BAZAR

C/ de Buenos Aires 5
L'Eixample ③
+34 635 66 20 35
hinojobazar.com

Eco-driven and tastefully put together, Hinojo flies the flag for zero-waste homewares (things like reusable glass spray bottles and wooden dustpan and brushes). But there's plenty for visitors to the city, too, like ethical perfumes, locally made ceramic vases and swirly 60s-inspired screen prints.

182 COCÓ GRANEL

C/ de Sueca 60
L'Eixample ③
+34 653 85 81 71

Find next level pantry essentials at Cocó Granel: turquoise spirulina tagliatelle, wasabi sesame seeds and whole-wheat spelt pasta, all sold by the gram. Don't leave without a bottle of organic cava and a jar of handmade granola made with Valencian honey, linseeds and dehydrated local oranges.

183 MÍMATE ORGANIC

C/ de Sueca 17
L'Eixample ③
+34 667 61 33 97
mimateorganic.com

Need sunblock? Pick up a jar from Mímate: it's mineral, vegan, and basically the Rolls Royce of eco-friendly suncream. Their skin care is divine, too. Lavender soap, solid shampoo, and conditioner is made by hand in Barcelona, and moisturisers (made by Italian brand Oway) are totally plastic-free.

184 QUART DE KILO

C/ de Quart 72
Extramurs ④
+34 633 22 95 79
quartdekilo.es

Found at the foot of the enormous Gothic defence towers Torres de Quart, this health food store sells planet-friendly products. Their chocolate selection is especially brilliant: pick up vegan bars with pistachio, almond and walnut, or 55% milk chocolate with almonds, oranges and sesame seeds.

185 DESANTATERESA

C/ de Salamanca 40
L'Eixample ③
+34 655 09 69 92
desantateresa.com

Aromatherapy is at the heart of this holistic operation, a dreamy refuge of designer candles and sustainable skincare. They also host wellness workshops which use the spoils of the shop to maximum effect. Expect events like guided meditation, which aim to tap into higher vibrations.

5 ace **MARKETS**
that aren't Mercat Central

186 **MERCAT MUNICIPAL DEL CABANYAL**

C/ de Martí Grajales 4
Poblats Maritims ⑧
+34 601 18 81 88
mercadocabanyal.es

Tables groan with cherry-red prawns and tanks of lobsters while old ladies push their way to the front at this busy market in the old fishing *barrio* of Cabanyal. Over 150 stalls jostle for attention, and the tables outside are filled with farmers selling vegetables straight from the fields.

187 **MERCADO ROJAS CLEMENTE**

Plaça de Rojas
Clemente
Extramurs ④
+34 963 52 54 78

A local crowd comes to this brilliant market to shop in peace and feast on *bocadillos* from the cafe. The small, select line-up serves artisan coffee, craft beer and muddy organic vegetables from the farms nearby. It's easy to spot: look for the big murals of flamingos and flowers.

188 **MERCAT MOSSÉN SORELL**

Plaça de Mossén
Sorell
Ciutat Vella ①
+34 962 08 47 36

The usual rosy Valencian tomatoes and enormous watermelons are on sale here, but this glass-walled market in El Carmen is also popular for its bars and cafes. Come for olives, pickles and vermouth, or a bottle of Valencian Bobal, from the experts at Vinostrum.

189 MERCAT MUNICIPAL JERUSALEM

C/ del Matemàtic
Marzal 2
Extramurs ④
+34 963 286 936

Locals who've been coming to this old-fashioned arcade for decades gossip with traders over meticulously arranged peaches. Hungry? There's an incredible cafe hidden at the back. In the morning it's full to the brim – spot rushed waiters with plates of *bocadillos* stacked up to their elbows.

190 MERCAT DE RUSSAFA

Plaça del Baró
de Cortés
L'Eixample ③
+34 963 74 40 25
mercatderussafa.com

This local market is smaller and quieter than Mercat Central but still packs a punch. It shows off the same pyramids of blushing pink tomatoes and local oranges. Bar Mercado de Ruzafa has been slinging *chivitos* since 1973. Brave visitors should hit up Insectum to snack on smoked crickets.

5 of the prettiest
POTTERY STUDIOS

---

191 MISC.

C/ del Pintor
Gisbert 21
L'Eixample ③

Part studio part shop, this dreamy space sporadically opens its doors to curious shoppers. DM for an appointment and pick up one-of-a-kind vases, illustrations and tableware. Spot artist and owner Lola Beltrán (and her four-legged assistant Peggy) making playful pieces with bold motifs.

192 CUIT

C/ de Cuba 62
L'Eixample ③
+34 651 55 59 33
cuit.es

Russafa is dotted with ceramics studios, but this is one of the biggest and best. Patricia Soriano and Celia Collado clearly have great taste; the interior is chic and shelves are filled with minimal, very usable pieces. Feeling inspired? Make your own tableware set on a whirlwind two-day course.

193 PLOU ESTUDI

C/ de la Corona 41
Ciutat Vella ①

On the fringes of El Carmen, ceramicist Elena López Lanzarote dances between running workshops and greeting visitors. Part of the shop is dedicated to local artists who exhibit and sell their work. Half-day mug building courses are fun for even the least arty folk.

194 OLMO

C/ de Millars 8
Jesús ④
+34 676 54 98 23
escuelafictile.com

Macarena Mompó has trained many a potter in Valencia from her studio, and she throws a mean vase. Pop in to buy her refined, expertly made ceramics hot from the kiln. Feeling brave? Get behind the wheel on a four-hour intensive *bautismo de torno* and see how you fare.

195 ANA ILLUECA

C/ de Rodrigo de
Pertegás 42
Camins al Grau ⑦
+34 645 20 26 26
anaillueca.com

Ana was one of the first on Valencia's new wave ceramicists, and she may well be one of the friendliest. Only the most determined make it to her studio in an un-hipster corner of La Creu del Grau. Your reward? A blinding line-up of tiles, bowls and cups overflowing with personality.

5 OLD SHOPS

where time stands still

---

196 LA TENDA ACAMPA SCOUT

C/ de la Llotja 8
Ciutat Vella ②
+34 963 91 46 96

Behind La Lonja, this twee scout shop could have been dreamt up by Wes Anderson. Glass cabinets on antique wooden doors display colourful scout badges while striped scarves hang like candy canes along the ceiling. Pay a visit and award yourself a 'local knowledge' badge.

197 TIENDA DE LAS OLLAS DE HIERRO

C/ dels Drets 4
Ciutat Vella ②
+34 963 92 20 24
tiendadelasollas
dehierro.com

Founded in 1793, Las Ollas is the oldest shop in Valencia, named after the pots it used to sell from Marseille. From the black and white chequered floors to the wooden shelves which reach the ceiling, every crevice is filled with gold brooches, hand-embroidered scarves, exquisite glass beads and religious items.

198 ENCUADERNACIONES LLORENS

C/ dels Cavallers 7
Ciutat Vella ①
+34 963 91 06 00

Bartolomé Llorens Tarrasa started this bookbinding and restoration business in 1882 on Calle de Bordadores, before moving to this shop on Carrer dels Cavallers. Fifth-generation bookbinder José works in a fascinating library of impeccably bound tomes and antique tools.

199 ABANICOS VIBENCA

Plaça de Lope de
Vega 5
Ciutat Vella ②
+34 690 19 20 55
abanicosvibenca.es

Vicente Benlloch Caballer learnt the art of fan-painting from his grandad and keeps his dream alive in this dapper shop. Find the rear window on Carrer de Martin Mengod to watch the master at work – one day he's customising fans with a client's beloved pet, the next he's splashing paint Pollock-style across the leaves.

200 SOMBREROS ALBERO

Plaça del Mercat 9
Ciutat Vella ②
+34 963 91 65 17
sombrerosalbero.es

Since it launched in 1820, this traditional millinery has founded another eight stores around Spain, but the original and the best is on Plaça del Mercat. Behind the retro façade find the classic panama, Texas cowboy hats and vintage bathing caps. Personalised sun hats sell like hot cakes.

197 TIENDA DE LAS OLLAS

5 of the coolest
RECORD SHOPS

201 K&H VINYL STORE

C/ del Doctor
Sumsi 21
L'Eixample ③
+34 960 61 56 31
www.khvinylstore.com

There's an unbelievable range of dance music sold here, from trippy Swiss house to hard-to-find Polish acid, all available across vinyl, CDs, cassette and MP3s. After hours it turns into a hush-hush club called Killing Time, where DJs play under-the-radar gigs in the dark, faintly cigarette-scented space.

202 ULTRASOUND

C/ de Cuba 49
L'Eixample ③
+34 960 06 82 38

Pop, rock and funk are the order of the day in this polished record shop in the throngs of Russafa. Their record selection is varied and vast, pick out a disc and pop it on the turntables to give it a listen. DJs play on their nifty set-up at the front of the store, expect 1980s rock marathons and house bangers.

203 DISCOS OLDIES

C/ de la Mare de Déu
de Gràcia 6
Ciutat Vella ②
+34 963 51 89 97

Discos Oldies might look like a 70s-time warp but they never stop improving on their eclectic stash, which ranges from Japanese jazz to cumbia to American rock. They have excellent taste, and pick out their favourite events of the month to share on Instagram – follow to find the best gigs and club nights.

204 DEVIL RECORDS

C/ Cerrajeros 5
Ciutat Vella ②

An inordinate amount of rock and punk records are squished into this tiny space, and vintage band t-shirts like Red Hot Chilli Peppers and Nirvana hang along the stairs like bunting. These guys know their stuff; they've released records including Malaga punk outfit Guiri Resort and the pop-rock group Heatwave.

205 HARMONY DISCOS

Passatge Doctor
Serra 9
L'Eixample ③
+34 963 52 18 39
harmony-discos.
negocio.site

Harmony Discos is a cornerstone for rock fans in the city. Behind the retro yellow storefront, every surface is covered in some kind of rock memorabilia, from stickers to band T-shirts. Expect a wide line-up of death metal, punk, hardcore, from Soen to Queens of the Stone Age.

5 fairy-tale
BOOKSHOPS
to get lost in

206 BANGARANG

C/ de l'Historiador
Diago 9
Extramurs ④
+34 601 48 24 09
bangarangcomics.com

A hip, well-read crowd heads to this boundary-pushing library to join book groups, take a creative writing workshop, listen to gastro-literary talks or find a new favourite magazine. The selection of classics is vast, but the comic book selection (graphic novels by Ana Penyas are ace) underpins the whole operation.

207 LETRAS Y VINOS

C/ del Músic
Belando 15
Benimaclet ⑥
+34 960 71 99 44
letrasyvinos.com

Benimaclet locals fiercely support their bookshop-meets-bar, and any event here is usually full to the rafters, with folks spilling out onto the pretty pedestrianised streets. They have a killer combination: large glasses of *garnacha* go incredibly well with a good book and a pianist playing Yann Tiersen classics.

208 LA BATISFERA

C/ de la Reina 167
Poblats Maritims ⑧
+34 962 04 58 45

Named after a 1930's submarine, this seaside bookshop is the place to dive into novels, explore lesser-known poetry and rub shoulders with the authors at meet and greet events. Peckish? The laidback cafe serves an excellent mint julep and beautifully presented nibbles, like langoustine tacos and cheese boards.

209 RAMON LLULL

C/ de la Corona 5
Ciutat Vella ①
+34 963 69 72 99
llibreriaramonllull.com

This highly-regarded bookshop was named the best in Spain in 2022 for its contribution to the literary scene. It stocks a stellar line-up of page-turners, from the poems of Bertolt Brecht to the ethereal short stories by Clara Pastor, and hosts loads of events from reading clubs to seminars and workshops.

210 RAFAEL SOLAZ

C/ de Sant Ferran 7
Ciutat Vella ②
+34 963 91 91 78
llibreriarafaelsolaz.es

Shelves buckling with books reach the wonky wooden beams of this store. Squeeze past weathered spines and gold lettering to find Rafael sifting through dusty boxes of old diaries and antique photographs. Ask him about the books that his dad wrote on the history of Valencia.

5 *fascinating*
ANTIQUES STORES

211 ANTIGÜEDADES ART DECO

C/ del Miracle 13
Ciutat Vella ①
+34 660 26 11 43

There are real treasures to be found in this spellbinding shop, where tightly-packed curios are balanced one on top of the other, from ceramic teapots to worn-in leather suitcases to the most brilliant retro coffee tins. Find an edited selection of their wares at the regular antiques market at Mercat de Colón, too.

212 PANNONICA VINTAGE

C/ de Baix 13
Ciutat Vella ①
+34 696 95 10 55
*pannonicavintage.
wordpress.com*

Only the very coolest 1950s furniture, art and nick-nacks find their way to Pannonica. The refined selection includes mid-century sideboards, UFO-shaped chrome lamps and Marcel Breuer's iconic Wassily chair. Looking for something smaller? Hunt down the vintage Dior sunglasses or the Louis Vuitton weekend bag.

213 STUDIO VINTAGE

C/ de la Puríssima 8
Ciutat Vella ①
+34 617 95 26 35
studiovintage.es

There's just a scant selection of furniture on display at Studio Vintage, but it's all drop-dead gorgeous. A mid-century sideboard here, an Ercol-style chair there. Items are hand-picked for their quality, so better nab that sublime, curvy mint-green sofa before it's gone forever.

214 RASTRO DE VALÈNCIA

Plaça de Amèlia
Chiner
Algirós ⑧

Dive into the chaos of this noisy flea market, where serious collectors haggle with hard-line traders over antique silverware and piles of battered books. With the lack of shade and over 300 stalls, it's not the most glamorous shopping experience, but for those who love a rummage it is a Sunday well spent.

215 NOËL RIBES

C/ de Vilaragut 7
Ciutat Vella ②
+34 646 72 80 32
noelribes.com

With a degree in art and archaeology and a diploma from Sotheby's, what Noël Ribes doesn't know about antiques could fit in a 17th-century marble mortar (there's one for sale here, conveniently). His small selection of *objets d'art* are known for their quality, pop in for fine Italian sculpture and Gothic iron door handles.

5 places to find the best
SPANISH PRODUCE

216 SIMPLE
C/ del Palau 5
Ciutat Vella ①
+34 963 92 50 22
simple.com.es

With its burgundy striped awning and displays of dried cotton and wicker baskets, Simple is more like a lifestyle shop than a food store, but their compact selection of Spanish-made produce is worth a gander. Sweets in delicately decorated tins, salt handmade in Ibiza and chocolate sardines are too pretty to be eaten.

217 FLOR DE CYNARA
C/ de Guillem
de Castro 58
Ciutat Vella ②
+34 667 41 84 49

The food from Extremadura, a western region of Spain bordering Portugal, doesn't get as much fame as it should. It's something that Shira de Torres (Cáceres) and Javier Vila (Valencia) want to change. Visit their deli and pick up extra virgin olive oil infused with truffle, dried figs from Almoharín and small-batch artisanal honey.

218 THE ESPANISTA
C/ de la Reina
Na Maria 9
L'Eixample ③
+34 630 54 04 09
theespanista.com

Daniel Martínez combines his love of tradition, food and art in his three shops. Excellent wine, vermouth, olive oil and locally made screen prints are here in abundance. Don't miss the mini library, with brilliant coffee table reads like the picture guide to houses in Cabanyal.

219 ORIGINAL CV

Plaça del Mercat 35
Ciutat Vella ②
+34 963 91 84 80
originalcv.es

Based opposite Mercat Central, Original CV crams antique pharmacy shelves with locally produced products. Gin flavoured with Valencian clementines by Fernandez Pons, Orange blossom-scented candles and black truffle oil made with Arbequina olives are among the goodies.

220 LEMBUTIC

C/ de les Comèdies 1
Ciutat Vella ②
+34 623 21 55 66
lembutic.com

Locals come to this store to stock up their pantry with extra special ingredients, like raw honey, fancy tinned fish (octopus in olive oil from the north of Spain or pickled Galician mussels) and stinky blue goat's cheese. Can't wait 'till you're home? They will open and serve any product on the upturned wine barrels outside.

5 picturesque
FLORISTS

221 FLOR DE LUNA

C/ del Pintor
Salvador Abril 11
L'Eixample ③
+34 662 29 87 28
flordelunaofficial.com

Jess and Kris, two friends from the Netherlands, offer a sustainable take on a florist, selling only dried flowers and grasses. Their chic shop is laden with wicker baskets full of bushy pampas, delicate autumnal-toned bouquets with dried daisies. Join a hoop workshop to make a *luna* of flowers to take home.

223 ABSOLUTA FLORA

222 KIOPU

C/ de la Concordia 4
Ciutat Vella ①
+34 634 36 68 07

As well as the usual petal-packed parcels, Kiopu has a huge range of hardy, low maintenance succulents and houseplants that are (almost) impossible to kill – good news for the not so green-fingered. Pick up a cactus for the balcony safe in the knowledge that it will survive the summer.

223 ABSOLUTA FLORA

C/ de Murillo 44
Ciutat Vella ①
+34 961 81 08 59
absolutaflora.com

A trip to New York was the inspiration for this modern, seasonal florist. Pick out all-white bunches of snowy flowers or go all out with an explosion of colour where blooms are painted every colour of the rainbow. Swoon at their selection of geometric candlesticks and vases, too.

224 ATELIER DE LA FLOR

C/ de Misser
Mascó 34
El Pla del Real ⑥
+34 963 25 60 67
atelierdelaflor.com

The love heart-red frontage of this florist hints at the romantic bunches that staff whip up inside. The sweetly scented shop is a riot of colour, from purple lavender wrapped in crinkly brown paper to bunches of powder-pink tulips to cascades of sunshine-yellow roses.

225 LA VIOLETA BY LOLÍN

Plaça de
l'Ajuntament,
Puesto 2
Ciutat Vella ②
+34 656 47 56 20
floreslavioleta.com

The Plaça de l'Ajuntament has a long history with flowers. In the 1920s Japanese-style pergolas sold blooms. Now, a cluster of traders carry on the tradition. Fancy a bouquet? Ask Lolín for a bunch, she's the third-generation owner of La Violeta, her grandma Teresa founded it almost a century ago.

5 BOUTIQUES and DESIGNERS
you need to know about

226 SIMUERO
C/ de Borriana 44
L'Eixample ③
+34 640 18 13 72
simuero.com

Rocío y Jorge started Simuero during lockdown and it took off like a rocket. Their chunky pieces look like long-lost treasures that have washed up on the beach. Email info@simuero.com and book an appointment to try on big gold pendants and wobbly silver rings and immediately fall in love.

227 CANDELA EN RAMA
C/ de Carrasquer 10
Ciutat Vella ①
+34 613 02 42 96
candelaenrama.com

The simplicity of the Mediterranean was Candela's inspiration for this stunning jeweller in the old town. Inside, terracotta tiles and whitewashed walls set the scene for gold pendants marked with wriggly lines like the rings of a tree trunk and dainty rings made up of tiny gold seeds, inspired by the rice fields of the Albufera.

228 LACONTRA
C/ de Cadis 38
L'Eixample ③
+34 960 08 35 16
lacontraroom.com

The sharp styles of Lacontra are a breath of fresh air in vintage-dominated Russafa. They're committed to working with brands that prioritise sustainability, and stock modern goods like bright jumpsuits by Barcelona's Thinking Mu, or waffle-soled daps by Slovakia's Novesta.

229 **STRAP**

Av. de Blasco
Ibáñez 33
El Pla del Real ⑥
+34 961 47 57 10
wearestrap.com

There is only one place to get the latest drop of Salomon or Mizuno in Valencia: Strap. Next to a noisy dual carriageway, ethereal hip hop plays out over a pin-sharp streetwear/skatewear line-up: Hélas denim, crisp Clarks Wallabees, and Carhartt WIP graphic tees. Founder Marc Strap often pops up at the best house nights, too.

230 **ESPAI SOLIDARIA**

C/ d'Alacant 27
L'Eixample ③
+34 961 14 92 40
juntosporlavida.org

Juntos por la Vida is a charity that works in Spain, Ukraine and Africa to make people's lives better, and this is one of the ways they raise money. The shop sells reworked clothes, childrenswear and bags made by their women's empowerment project in Benin. Learn how to sew and design in personalised workshops.

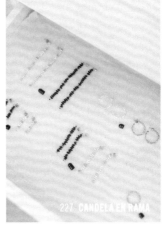

227 CANDELA EN RAMA

5 shops for unique
BAGS *and* SHOES

---

231 **ONA NEGRA**

C/ de la Nau 7
Ciutat Vella ②
+34 960 09 46 85
onanegra.com

Fans of rebellious shoe styles will adore Ona Negra, a small but stylish joint that serves up brands like Act, a Berlin-Mallorca based brand that makes edgy ballet flats and Kosma, a Menorca-based brand specialising in cute-yet-practical heels. In the market for a new bag? Their canvas shoppers, made in Spain, are very tempting.

231 ONA NEGRA

232 OOBUKA

C/ d'Arolas 7
Ciutat Vella ②
+34 961 94 61 33

Sheets of supple leather get moulded, cut and sewn into the most incredible totes, backpacks and wallets in the Oobuka studio. Between huge rolls of canvas and some industrial-looking sewing machines, there are one-off rucksacks, make-to-measure bicycle bags, and leather-bottomed weekend bags.

233 PÁNGALA

C/ de Na Jordana 2
Ciutat Vella ①
+34 676 09 47 82
pangala.es

Owner Almudena is usually found sewing in her sunny corner of El Carmen, whipping up custom-order rucksacks and listening to an audiobook before nipping over to greet visitors. Most bags are made with a water-resistant paper, which she combines in fantastically named colourways like *pan con tomate*.

234 ALEJANDRA MONTANER

C/ de Sorní 30
L'Eixample ③
+34 963 33 21 17
alejandramontaner.com

On a quiet street in La Gran Via, this boutique sells elegant brands from around the world, which tap into a laidback, bohemian style. Buy chunky chocolate-brown Blundstone boots for stomping through the streets in winter, or delicately hand-woven sandals in sage green and red to keep toes cool in the summer.

235 ALPARGATERÍA SANCHIS

C/ de Cervantes 6
Extramurs ④
+34 963 52 19 68
alpargateriavalencia.es

Espardenyes or *alpargatas* are traditional sandals with origins (some believe) in ancient Egyptian times. They're seen from southern France to Mexico, but Spain is perhaps best known for sporting them. Visit to try on the *alpargata Valenciana de careta*, with white canvas and black laces.

ESPAI VERD

35 BUILDINGS TO ADMIRE

5 examples of
MODERN and BRUTALIST
architecture

---

236 LA RAMBLETA

C/ de Pius IX 2
Jesús ④
+34 960 01 15 11
larambleta.com

This seven-storey concrete box might look big and bolshy, but take in the surroundings and notice how it fuses the housing blocks and parkland. The idea of La Rambleta was not to dominate, but to build community. Events are varied and accessible, from puppet theatre to Pink Floyd tribute bands.

237 COLEGIO ALEMÁN

C/ de Jaume Roig 16
El Pla del Real ⑥

Form follows function at this working school, which has been noted and protected by El Colegio de Arquitectos de Valencia. Plans were drawn up for this Bauhaus-inspired building in Berlin, and it was completed in 1961. See the *Nolla* tiles on the front? They're a nod to Valencia's rich ceramic history.

238 ESPAI VERD

C/ del Músic Hipòlit
Martínez 16
Benimaclet ⑥

Antonio Cortés wanted to change the way that people lived with Espai Verd. Built in the 1980s, the radical space combines concrete, height and lush green space to incredible effect, like a modern-day Hanging Gardens of Babylon. Did it work? Peep through the gate at the fountains and trees, and judge for yourself.

239 MUSEU VALENCIÀ DE LA IL·LUSTRACIÓ I DE LA MODERNITAT

C/ de Quevedo 10
Ciutat Vella ②
+34 963 88 37 30
muvim.es

Concrete and glass are the two main players in this sleek gallery, designed by Guillermo Vázquez Consuegra. Opened in 2001 and set in a small, peaceful park, it houses a lively roster of exhibitions, including mediaeval pots and ceramics, contemporary typography and modern art.

240 TORRE DE RIPALDA

Plaça de la Legió
Espanyola 3
El Pla del Real ⑥

The winged balconies of the Ripalda Tower were inspired by a trip to Japan; they're pretty iconic in Valencia. When it was built in 1969 it was a marvel of modern architecture and the tallest building in the city, designed for the bourgeois to live in spacious flats which blended indoors and outdoors.

5 *stunning*
MODERNISMO
VALENCIANO *buildings*

241 **EDIFICI DE CORREUS**

Plaça de
l'Ajuntament 24
Ciutat Vella ②
+34 963 51 23 70

Grander than your average post office, the immense Edifici de Correus was built in 1922 to symbolise the progress and innovation made by mail and telegraphs in the 20th century. Marvel at the enormous domed glass ceiling – those coats of arms circled around the edge represent the 48 provinces of Spain.

242 ESTACIÓ DEL NORD

C/ d'Alacant 25
L'Eixample ③

In line with Art Nouveau, Valencian Modernism often celebrates the city's own identity, with motifs like oranges, *falleras*, fishing, and agriculture. The best example of this is Estació del Nord. Inside, find the beautifully tiled vestibule, ornate wooden ticket booths and intricate mosaics.

243 PASATGE DE RIPALDA

C/ de Sant Vicent
Màrtir / Plaça de
Marià Benlliure
Ciutat Vella ②

Somewhat dilapidated, this covered arcade is often used as a shortcut, but it's worth a second look. Built in 1889, it was inspired by the glamorous Italian neoclassical shopping arcades. The glass ceiling is especially beautiful, and it's rumoured that the semi-circular windows on the wall were made by Gaudí.

244 MERCAT CENTRAL DE VALÈNCIA

Plaça de la Ciutat
de Bruges
Ciutat Vella ②
+34 963 82 91 00
mercadocentral valencia.es

Designed in 1914 by Francisco Guardia and Alejandro Soler, this market is crowned with a grand domed iron and glass ceiling. Locals and visitors weave through 274 stalls loaded with fruit and vegetables (48.000 kg is unloaded every day), and more hanging *jamón* legs than there are baubles on a Christmas tree.

245 EDIFICI GÓMEZ I

C/ de la Pau 31
Ciutat Vella ②

With its ornate balconies and romantic turret, this residential building stops people in their tracks. It was built in 1902 by Francisco Mora Berenguer, who was among the first to study in the Barcelona School of Architecture. His friend Gaudí was a big influence, seen in this curvy, organic-looking masterpiece.

5 impossibly
O R N A T E *buildings*

---

246 **LA CASA JUDÍA**
C/ de Castelló 20
L'Eixample ③

This bright, joyful building, with its stylised art deco balconies and Egyptian-inspired columns, was built in 1930 by architect Francisco Guardiola for Yosef Shalóm. Spot the Star of David painted above the door; it's here that the city's Jewish community met secretly to celebrate Kabbalat Shabbat and other festivals.

247 **PALACIO DEL MARQUÉS DE DOS AGUAS**
C/ del Poeta Querol 2
Ciutat Vella ②

This rococo-style mansion is covered in swirly marble like a perfectly iced cake, and inside it's just as fabulous. The palace dates back to the 15th century, but it was given a Cinderella-style makeover in the 1740s. Inside, find a fascinating ceramics stash, and some palatial rooms.

248 **CATEDRAL DE VALÈNCIA**
Plaça de la Reina
Ciutat Vella ①

In 2004 Professor Carmen Pérez peeked through a hole in the false ceiling and found a masterpiece: a hidden fresco of angels. Painted in 1472, it took seven years to complete, and had been covered for hundreds more. It's one of the many fascinating sights here, from grand works of art to a Renaissance silver altarpiece.

249 CASA DEL PUNT DE GANXO

Plaça de l'Almoina 4
Ciutat Vella ①

Set on an elegant square, the swirling, leafy patterns on the rusty pink tiles and the delicate wrought iron balconies of Casa del Punt de Ganxo are a show-stopper. On the ground floor is the Chapel of San Valero, built in 1719 – spot the sculpture of Valero himself leaning over the lintel.

250 EDIFICI DELS DRACS

C/ de Sorní 4
L'Eixample ③

Built in 1901 by Valencian architect José Manuel Cortina Pérez, this building could feature in *Game of Thrones* with the amount dragons crawling on its façade. The neo-Gothic structure is an imposing presence on a busy shopping street, yet most people are completely oblivious to the coiled creatures holding up giant columns.

247 PALACIO DEL MARQUÉS DE DOS AGUAS

252 LA FINCA ROJA

5 buildings with a
HIDDEN STORY

251 **BANYS DE L'ALMIRALL**
C/ dels Banys
de l'Almirall 3-5
Ciutat Vella ①
+34 618 22 24 38
banysalmirall.gva.es

When Valencia was under Moorish reign, the city would have been filled with bath houses. Now, the only remaining example is the Banys de l'Almirall. Interestingly, it belongs to an Arab tradition, but it was built nearly 100 years after the Christian conquest. Visit and start wishing the walls could talk.

252 **LA FINCA ROJA**
C/ de Jesús 75
Extramurs ④

A great example of rational architecture, La Finca Roja offered Valencia's working class a more middle-class lifestyle. It was the only development in the area when it was built in 1929, and for designer Enrique Viedma Vidal, it was a utopian vision: 378 apartments around one sociable courtyard.

253 EL ALMUDÍN

Plaça de Sant Lluís
Bertran 2
Ciutat Vella ①
+34 962 08 45 21

This art gallery and venue has a secret past life. Dating back to the 14th century, it was the old grain store of the city, one of the most important trades of the time. Inside, spot the old paintings of the patron saints who watched over the precious cargo. Now the space is used for live music and exhibitions.

254 REAL COLEGIO SEMINARIO DE CORPUS CHRISTI

C/ de la Nau 2
Ciutat Vella ②
+34 963 51 41 76
patriarcavalencia.es

Archbishop of Valencia Juan de Ribera (1532-1611) was a controversial figure. He wanted priests to be trained to a tee, so he built this college, right next to the university, to battle their scientific secularism. Inside, find a museum and gallery cocooned in sublime Renaissance architecture.

255 TORRES DE QUART

Plaça de Santa
Úrsula 1
Ciutat Vella ①
+34 618 80 39 07
*valencia.es/-/
infociudad-torres-
de-quart*

Built between 1441 and 1460, Torres de Quart is one of the old doors of the mediaeval walls of the city. On 28 of June 1808 the *Primera Batalla de Valencia* took place, and the canons of Napoleonic troops commanded by Marshal Moncey pounded the doors. Visit today and you may see birds nesting in the craters.

SANTIAGO CALATRAVA's
5 best works in the city

---

256 LA CIUTAT DE LES ARTS I LES CIÈNCIES

Av. del Professor
López Piñero 7
Quatre Carreres ⑦
+34 961 97 46 86
cac.es

This project by Calatrava took nearly a decade to build. Some suggest it went four times over budget, around 1,2 billion. The buildings speak about nature and their environment; L'Hemisfèric looks like a fish with its reflection in the water, and Palau de les Arts looks like a futuristic boat sailing out to sea.

257 PONT L'ASSUT DE L'OR

Quatre Carreres ⑦

The trademark of this bridge that spans the Túria next to La Ciutat de les Arts i les Ciències is a dynamic pylon that reaches 125 metres into the sky. Its name harks back to the Túria's days as a rapid river; the word *assut* is a mechanism used to regulate the flow of a river, like a weir.

258 PONT DE L'EXPOSICIÓ

El Pla del Real ⑥

There's something quite comforting about the gently curved underbelly of this bridge (also known as Alameda Bridge) – perhaps that's why so many outdoor fitness and dance groups choose to meet here. Built between 1991 and 1995, the tied arch bridge features two poles that swoop over the Túria park, stretching over 130 metres.

259 ALAMEDA METRO STATION

Passeig de la Ciutadella
El Pla del Real ⑥

Below Pont de l'Exposició (or Alameda Bridge) there are glass diamonds on the floor – a clue that there's something special in the metro station below. Inside Alameda station, with its vaulted roof like ribs, are Calatrava's trademark shimmery mosaic tiles. It's illuminated by those diamond lightwells and playfully dappled by the shadows of people's feet.

260 PONT DEL NOU D'OCTUBRE

Campanar ⑤

From Alameda it's a short tram ride to one of Calatrava's first works in Valencia – and possibly one of his best. Built between 1986 and 1989 by the burgeoning new architect, there are subtle signs of his iconic style. Space age fences, fluid shapes, abstract sculptures that look like moody crows.

The 5 most
STUNNING CHURCHES

261 **ESGLÉSIA DE SANTA CATERINA**

Plaça de Santa
Caterina 8
Ciutat Vella ②
+34 963 91 77 13

The arches of Santa Caterina were filled by architect Rubio Mulet in the 1740s during a renovation. He wanted to get rid of some rubble and used it to plug up the holes – among it was a statue of a bishop. Look for the poor guy's head in the middle archway.

261 ESGLÉSIA DE SANTA CATERINA

262 ESGLÉSIA DE SANT JOAN DE L'HOSPITAL

C/ del Trinquet
de Cavallers 5
Ciutat Vella ②
+34 963 92 29 65
sanjuandelhospital.es

Founded in 1238, this is the oldest church in Valencia and also the most peaceful. From the outside it looks like another apartment block, but slip through the big double doors to discover a welcoming church and quiet courtyard lined with ancient alcoves, once used to shelter the sick for the onsite hospital.

263 ESGLÉSIA DE SANT NICOLAU

C/ dels Cavallers 35
Ciutat Vella ①
+34 963 91 33 17
sannicolasvalencia.com

Known as Valencia's Sistine Chapel, this church is painted top to toe in splendid baroque frescoes. Now, the attraction gets very busy, with queues forming at peak times. Is it worth it? Absolutely – and the headphone-guided tour blocks out the sound of the crowds.

264 ESGLÉSIA DE SANT ESTEVE PROTOMÀRTIR

Plaça de Sant
Esteve 2
Ciutat Vella ①
+34 963 91 82 76
*sanesteban
protomartir.es*

If the crowds of Sant Nicolau are too much, this small church is a quieter local's spot, but it's still utterly gorgeous. The Gothic church was spruced up in the 18th century with intricate plasterwork and powder-blue William Morris-esque patterns splashed across the walls and ceiling.

265 BASÍLICA DE LA MARE DE DÉU DELS DESEMPARATS

Plaça de la Verge
Ciutat Vella ①
+34 963 91 92 14
*basilicade
samparados.org*

The seashell-pink walls and azure domed roof of this baroque church are one of the prettiest sights in the city. It's the home of the patron saint of Valencia, La Verge de Déu dels Desemparats, whose slightly bent posture means locals lovingly nickname her *geperudeta* (hunchback).

5 buildings that are
OUT OF THIS WORLD

---

266 LA ANTIGUA BODEGA VINIVAL

Camí Fondo 3
Alboraia ⑧

At the end of Patacona is a cluster of enormous, abandoned towers with little portholes. They are the wacky old wine-making facilities of Vinival, built during a wine boom in 1969 with a capacity of 32 million litres. They've since been recognised for their architectural merit, and rumours are flying about their regeneration.

267 TORRE MIRAMAR

Rotonda Av. de
Catalunya
Benimaclet ⑥

Known as the most expensive roundabout in Valencia, this 2009 project was supposed to be a viewing tower to look at the sea. The look-out was closed permanently after three months when they realised that it offered spectacular views of the motorway, tower blocks and car parks. It cost 24 million euro.

268 OCEANOGRÀFIC

C/ d'Eduardo Primo
Yúfera
Quatre Carreres ⑦
+34 960 47 06 47
oceanografic.org

Aquariums will always be a controversial topic (this is the biggest in Europe), but architecturally speaking it's a stunner. The exaggerated, undulating fins of the *Edifici Oceanogràfic* were designed by Félix Candela to make visitors feel enveloped by their watery surroundings.

269 VELES E VENTS

C/ Marina Real
Juan Carlos I
Poblats Maritims ⑧
+34 690 70 52 16
veleseventsvalencia.es

Designed by David Chipperfield, this clean-lined, zig-zagging structure was built in 2007 when Valencia hosted the sailing competition America's Cup. Its four shaded balconies were designed for spectators, and they still deliver hypnotising views of the port.

270 ESTUDIOS ANDRO

C/ Ciutat d'Eibar 2
Paterna
estudiosandro.es

This unusual office block was built in 1978 by a Valencian studio GO.DB, and it's found deep in the industrialised fringes of the city. Flanked by boring warehouses, the sleek building is topped with seemingly floating UFO-shaped rooms. Want to look inside? Grab lunch in the no-frills cafe downstairs, where you can peek at the hidden architectural flourishes.

269 VELES E VENTS

Sección 17
Sociedades

Sección
Fabricantes de
Aguardientes

MERCADO DE LA IMPRENTA

80 PLACES TO DISCOVER VALENCIA

5 surprising
SCULPTURES and
FOUNTAINS

---

271 POINTS OF VIEW
Rotonda Pont
de Montolivet
Quatre Carreres ⑦

This lustrous 3,8-ton sculpture rises up from a roundabout like a cartoon tornado. Made by British artist Tony Cragg for an exhibition in Valencia, it was bought and donated to the city by the Hortensia Herrero Foundation, an arts fund founded by the co-owner of Mercadona supermarket.

272 LA PAMELA
C/ Marina Real
Juan Carlos I
Poblats Maritims ⑧

Forgot your sun hat? This sculpture has you covered. Near the port, a featureless oversized head crafted by Valencian artist Manolo Valdés sports a wide-brimmed *pamela* hat offering shade to scorched visitors. Once again, the Hortensia Herrero Foundation is to thank for this installation.

273 DAMA IBÉRICA
Av. de les Corts
Valencianes 35
Benicalap ⑤

Another impressive sculpture by Valdés, this cobalt-blue head is made of 22.000 ceramic pieces and stands over 20 metres tall. Built in 2007, it's an homage to the *Dama de Elche* – a revered 4th-century artefact that was stumbled upon by a 14-year-old in L'Alcúdia, Valencia.

274 NAU DE L'AIGUA

C/ de Pavia 89
Poblats Marítims ⑧

Just a few steps from Cabanyal beach, minimal metal frames sketch the outline of a Catalan boat. It's a nod to the area's rich fishing history and the traditional boats that would have lined this shore – the *barrio* was founded by families who began fishing these waters in the 13th century.

275 FUENTE DE LA PANTERA ROSA

C/ de les Filipines 39
L'Eixample ③

Squint and this tall fountain with a rusty oxidised surface and triangular head might look a bit like the Pink Panther. At least that's what the council of 1997 thought, so they went ahead and painted it pink. In 2018 it was painted red again – designer Miquel Navarro's preferred colour.

272 LA PAMELA

5 chilled things to do when it's
TOO HOT

---

276 DIVE INTO PISCINA LA HÍPICA

C/ de Genaro
Lahuerta Pintor 10
La Saïdia ⑥
+34 963 61 53 63
lahipica.com

Only locals and tipped-off visitors know that the pool of this equestrian club is open to the public; they roll out towels on the grassy banks and sip a *tinto de verano* before diving into cool turquoise water. Families note: rubber rings might be required as it's very deep with no shallow end.

277 SHOP AT CENTRO COMERCIAL SALER

Av. del Professor
López Piñero 16
Quatre Carreres ⑦
+34 963 95 70 12
ccsaler.com

It's not the most enriching social activity, but when the sun is set to scorching this shopping centre is a safe bet to escape the heat. El Saler has a cinema (with matinée screenings), supervised play area, arcade, and a compact line-up of high street brands like Zara and Mango.

278 HIRE A GO-KART
FROM: FLEXI BIKES
AND BOATS
AT: CIUTAT DE LES ARTS I
LES CIÈNCIES
Quatre Carreres ⑦
+34 605 32 19 16

The Ciutat de les Arts i les Ciències
swims in a network of ice-blue pools,
for some reason it makes it seem cooler.
Potter around them in a go-kart – there
are four-seaters with a parasol to keep
UVs at bay – available to hire from Flexi
Bikes and Boats, between Hemisfèric and
L'Umbracle.

279 TAKE A BOAT TRIP
WITH: CATAMARAN HAPPY
Marina Norte
Poblats Marítims ⑧
+34 620 76 82 91
catamaranhappy.com

Catamaran Happy has a small fleet of
red and white boats on the marina that
even the biggest landlubber can pilot,
no licence required. Groups of up to six
can commandeer a boat, kitted out with
an ice box for beers, GPS, and awnings
to protect sailors from that pesky sun.

280 SPLASH AT PISCINA BENICALAP
C/ d'Andreu Alfaro
Benicalap ⑤
+34 963 82 20 54
aquaval.es

Kids and adults alike love a good splash
at this water park. Toddlers paddle in the
ankle-depth play area with mushrooms
that squirt water while big kids whizz
down toboggans into the deep pool.
The restaurant serves basic burgers and
pizza, but picnics are allowed too. Tip:
book a VIP area for extra shade.

The 5 best squares for
PEOPLE WATCHING

---

281 PLAÇA DEL MERCAT
Ciutat Vella ②

With views of Mercat Central and La Lonja, this is one of the most picturesque *plaças* – it's also flush with history. There's been a market of some sort here since the 13th century, it was used as a site for bull fights, and in the 15th century it was where public executions took place.

281 PLAÇA DEL MERCAT

282 PLAÇA DE L'AJUNTAMENT
Ciutat Vella ②

The monks were presumably peeved when their monastery was used as barracks in 1835, then knocked down in 1892. It freed up space for the city's biggest square, flanked by flower stalls and a grand town hall. Bars and restaurants are good for people watching, but the best views are from the town hall balcony.

283 PLAÇA DEL DOCTOR COLLADO
Ciutat Vella ②

People from all walks of life take up a seat in this colourful terrace, from holidaymakers sipping beers at Blanquita Bar to old fellas enjoying a leisurely *almuerzo* at Bar El Kiosko. See the antique clock on number five? It marks the old site of a famous watch specialist which dated back to the 18th century.

284 PLAÇA DE LA VERGE
Ciutat Vella ①

There is a constant flow of people through this coral-coloured square; visitors take selfies by the bronze fountain, children play on the steps of the basilica and office workers weave through the crowds. It is one of the prettiest squares in the city, and has been a *plaça* of sorts since the Roman era.

285 PLAÇA REDONDA
Ciutat Vella ②

It might look modern, but this circular square was built by Salvador Escrig in 1840. Back then there were characterful shop signs, fruit stalls and wobbly balconies. Some still haven't forgiven the 2012 renovation for stripping that away, but it's a unique place to visit nonetheless.

5 fun squares that
COME TO LIFE AT NIGHT

---

286 PLAÇA DEL XÚQUER
Algirós ⑦

This sleepy, tree-filled square wakes up at night. Indie bars like Rocafull blast out The Cure and dish out very generous gin and tonics. Across the *plaça*, La Vitti hosts offbeat jazz bands in their cosy bar, and La Salamandra Xuquer dishes out homemade vermouth.

287 PLAÇA DEL NEGRET
Ciutat Vella ①

A bohemian crowd head to Plaça del Negret to hang out and chat 'til the small hours. It was the site of the first public drinking fountain in the city in 1850, topped with the statue of a child. Locals called it *el negrito* due to the colour of metal used, a nickname that became official in 1940.

288 PLAÇA DE CÁNOVAS DEL CASTILLO
L'Eixample ③

This grand square is where well-heeled residents come to cut loose. Order a 45-day matured steak and a Mallorcan cheese board at Can Valear, graze on sharing boards of *jamón* and chorizo at El Cauce, and party until sunrise at Havana, a club for sharp outfits and champagne on ice.

289 PLAÇA DEL CEDRE
Algirós ⑦

Just across the road from the polytechnic campus, a lively university group sips beers at Plaça del Cedre. The leafy square has laidback drinking dens: there's the loosely London-themed Underground Café Pub with its cheap drinks and foosball table, cheesy tunes at Pub Ibiza, and affordable cocktails at Café Colores.

290 PLAÇA DEL TOSSAL
Ciutat Vella ①

The route is well-trodden to this crowded square, which literally lights up with clubs and bars on its perimeter. By day visit the Tossal Gallery, where among modern art important parts of the Islamic city walls are displayed. By night, drink margaritas on the terrace of La Tia Juana and watch the madness unfold.

287 PLAÇA DEL NEGRET

5 places with
STUNNING VIEWS

---

291 **EL MICALET**
AT: CATEDRAL
DE VALÈNCIA
**Plaça de la Reina
Ciutat Vella** ①
catedraldevalencia.es

Cling to a wiry rail as the 207 steps get
gradually steeper and the ceiling coils
tighter in this Gothic-style bell tower.
Built between 1381 and 1424, up on the
terrace there are incredible views and
a 7,5-tonne bell which strikes deafeningly
on the hour.

294 TORRES DELS SERRANS

292 TORRE DE SANTA CATALINA

AT: ESGLÉSIA DE
SANTA CATERINA
Plaça de Santa
Caterina 8
Ciutat Vella ②

It's not as tall or old as El Micalet, but this baroque tower is just as loved. Valero Viñes laid the first stone in 1688, but after his death work was completed by his brother Juan Bautista Viñes in 1705. A stomp up the winding steps is the best way to appreciate the decades of work.

293 EL CORTE INGLÉS

C/ del Pintor
Maella 37
Camins al Grau ⑦
+34 963 35 05 00
elcorteingles.com

Not a fan of spiral staircases? A lift whisks architecture fans to the eighth-floor cafe of El Corte Inglés Avenida de Francia for aerial views of Ciutat de les Arts i les Ciències. The slightly dowdy department store restaurant with floor-to-ceiling windows is the unlikely viewing spot for L'Umbracle, L'Àgora and the Assut de l'Or.

294 TORRES DELS SERRANS

Plaça dels Furs
Ciutat Vella ①
+34 963 91 90 70

Not only does Torres dels Serrans offer great views, it's loaded with fascinating stories. From the 16th to the 19th century it was used as a prison (look for the bell on the side, it rang when someone escaped). During the Civil War, artwork from Madrid's Museo del Prado was stashed here.

295 MIRADOR DE AVES SALER

Playa del Saler
El Saler

Good views aren't always high up. This secluded look-out on the beach of Saler is a place to unplug and settle into the sea breeze while testing your twitching skills. Walk along wooden decks that weave through the dunes before spotting grebes, swamphens and warblers, if you're lucky.

5 spots with the prettiest
TILES

296 TASKA LA REINA

C/ de la Reina 173
Poblats Maritims ⑧
+34 961 52 76 86
restaurantecabanyal-
taskalareina.com

This seafood bar really bagged a winner in the exquisitely tiled house on Carrer de la Reina. Inside it's not quite as picture-perfect, but their menu of seafood-centred Mediterranean tapas is decent. Choose from squidgy figs with smoked sardines, grilled clams or steamed Galician cockles.

297 MUSEO CASA NATALICIA DE SAN VICENTE FERRER

C/ del Mar 51
Ciutat Vella ②
+34 963 52 84 81
casa-natalicia-san-
vicente-ferrer.
webnode.es

It's said that Vicente Ferrer Miguel was nine years old when he touched the wounds of a boy and they disappeared. The saint was born in Valencia in 1350 in this spot – although the house itself has been rebuilt. Tile fans will love the vestibule, covered in Manises ceramics which depict Vicente's miracles.

298 PALAU DE CERVELLÓ

Plaça de Tetuán 3
Ciutat Vella ②
+34 963 52 54 78

Built for the Cervelló family in the 18th century and home to kings during the 19th century, it's not surprising that the interiors of this palace are over the top. The first floor has been dressed to imitate the original decor – spot upholstered walls, silver tea sets, and hand-painted tiles throughout.

299 MUSEU DE CERÀMICA DE MANISES

C/ Sagrario 22
Manises
+34 961 52 10 44
museumanises.es

Serious ceramics geeks will adore this exhaustive museum, which follows the story of Valencian pottery. Follow the evolution of the signature metallic glaze, admire the handiwork of 14th-century hand-painted tiles, and see where modern potters are going with the annual Manises National Ceramic Contest.

300 ESGLÉSIA DEL PATRIARCA

Plaça del Col·legi del Patriarca 189
Ciutat Vella ②
+34 963 51 41 76
patriarcavalencia.es

This chapel is part of the El Real Colegio Seminario de Corpus Christi, but there's no entrance fee here. The walls are embellished with the frescoes of Genoese painter Bartolomé Matarana, and the lovely geometric tiles wrap around the entire lower half of the chapel's walls.

5 places to
MAKE A DIFFERENCE

———

301 **SANAMARES**

Marine veterinarian Estíbaliz Parras founded Sanamares when she wanted to combine her love of the sea with her expertise. Their events range from workshops on how to be a more responsible surfer to weekend diving trips to study sea slugs and lectures on local biodiversity.

302 **OBSERVADORES DEL MAR**

observadoresdelmar.es

Observadores del Mar calls on the public to help contribute to data on research projects. For example, there's a gap in knowledge around birds at sea. Budding ornithologists can log seabirds they spot, which will be cross referenced with temperature, fishing and water salinity to get a better understanding of their behaviour.

303 MERCAT DE L'HORTA
C/ Martínez Ferrando
L'Eixample ③

Get freshly dug radishes and pocket-sized watermelons direct from the folks who grow them at Mercats de l'Horta. Set up to support local farmers, the weekly markets take place around the city, and the most central is every Tuesday morning next to Mercat de Colón. Terra i Xufa is our favourite stall – look out for their organic *horchata*.

304 BIOAGRADABLES
bioagradables.org

In 2012, five friends went to the beach and were shocked at how many bottles, plastic bags and cups they found. It was the start of BIOagradables, a not-for-profit group formed to protect Valencia's natural environment through action days and education. Join a beach clean-up, do your bit and have fun along the way.

305 RED CROSS
cruzroja.es

Red Cross is a neutral charity which helps people in need around the world, and they're pretty active across Valencia. Volunteers will need to complete an application form then attend an interview before they can join the team at festivals, help at litter picks, and clean up the countryside.

5 hands-on **WORKSHOPS** and **TOURS**

306 **NYÀS VIDRIO RECICLADO**

AT: VILLA INDIANO
Cami de l'Estació 4
Burjassot
nyasartesa.com

Give Mirella and Rafa an empty beer bottle and they'll transform it into a work of art. Leftover glass turns into picture frames, vases and terrariums with copper foil and a nifty soldering iron. Learn how to work their magic at one of their classes, usually held in the decadent surroundings of Villa Indiano.

307 **KONLAKALMA CERÁMICAS**

C/ del Nord 26
Extramurs ④
+34 680 22 58 05

Katrin's organic, billowy vases are all hand-built, meaning they are wonderfully asymmetrical and brimming with character. Can't commit to a three-month course? She shares her techniques in small, relaxing workshops – keep an eye out on her Instagram page.

308 **ENSEDARTE**

C/ de l'Estamenyeria
Vella 6
Ciutat Vella ②
+34 616 99 99 12
ensedarte.com

Many of Valencia's orange groves used to be filled with mulberry trees, and in the 18th century half of the city worked with silk in one way or another. Eva works wonders with silk, taking inspiration from Valencia's architecture and culture. Join a silk scarf workshop to give it a whirl.

309 MY FIRST PAELLA

C/ del Penyagolosa 5
L'Eixample ③
+34 626 09 08 79
myfirstpaella.es

They say paella should be cooked over an open fire, and (if we're being really picky) using orange wood. Failing that, try this beginner's course in Russafa – it takes a light-hearted approach to a dish that's taken very seriously. It even includes a morning trip to the market to pick up the ingredients.

310 CERVEZA TYRIS

AT: POLÍGONO INDUSTRIAL
FUENTE DEL JARRO
C/ Ciutat de Sevilla 16
Paterna
+34 961 06 40 50
cervezatyris.com

On a quiet industrial estate to the northwest of the city, local beer heroes Tyris have opened up their brewery to curious ale fans. Take the metro over, pop on a hair net and join a tour of their slick operation, before tasting five of their best brews in the tap room.

307 KONLAKALMA CERÁMICAS

5 essential
FALLAS sights

311 **MASCLETÁ**

Plaça de
l'Ajuntament
Ciutat Vella ②
visitvalencia.com/
agenda-valencia

Fireworks flood the streets and smoke fills
the air during Fallas, the festival in March
where hundreds of wooden sculptures are
placed in squares and burned, while men
and women dress in spectacular silk and
gold outfits. No one knows exactly when
it began, but some point to carpenters in
the Middle Ages who burned excess wood
on the eve of their patron saint. Mascletá
is one of its most-loved (and loudest)
events. Every day of the festival at 2 pm
an ear-splitting firework display takes
place at the town hall. Join the crowds
at the Plaça de l'Ajuntament and feel the
explosions rattle your bones.

312 **LA OFRENDA DE FLORES**

Plaça de la Verge
Ciutat Vella ①

During this beautiful ritual *falleras* and
falleros visit Plaça de la Verge to offer
flowers to a 15-metre-tall sculpture of
the Mare de Déu dels Desamparats. The
queue they form is enormous, and snakes
through the city. Some 100.000 bouquets
eventually form the *virgen*'s dress, laid by
plucky souls who climb the figure.

313 BUÑUELOS AND STREET FOOD

With Fallas comes the ravishing smell of deep-fried dough, thanks to the street food trucks on almost every corner. Try *churros* with nutella and crispy *buñuelos de calabaza* coated in sugar. Horchatería El Collado still pulls and shapes them by hand – during Fallas there's a queue a hundred *churros* long.

314 CAVALCADA DEL FOC

A traditional street parade, but make it Fallas. Onlookers look genuinely scared when they see angle grinders spitting sparks and dragons spewing flames haring down the road. It is a prelude to the end of Fallas, a call to go to the final bonfires. With flamethrowers like that, we're not going to argue.

315 LA CREMÀ

The atmosphere is red-hot at the Fallas finale. The wooden sculptures in the *plaças* are burnt, with the biggest in the Plaça de l'Ajuntament left until last, around 11 pm. Crowds squeeze in like *buñuelos* in a bag to the crackling spectacle and feel the heat of the flames warm their cheeks.

5 reasons to visit the
MUSEO DEL SILENCIO

AT: CEMENTERI GENERAL DE VALÈNCIA
C/ Santo Domingo De Guzmán 27
Jesús ④
+34 963 77 35 24
museodelsilencio.com

316 WOMEN WHO LEFT THEIR MARK

For Rafael Solaz, his local cemetery was a museum of hidden stories. His book *Museo del Silencio* tells its forgotten tales; find a copy and head to Cementeri General. Routes include *Women Who Left Their Mark*, which tells the story of the gifted poet Virginia Dotres who died just 15-years-old.

317 VALENCIAN PAINTER JOAQUÍN SOROLLA'S GRAVE

Can't find the book? Visitors can also follow cemetery signs (famous tombs are signposted) or email *sbalbastre@valencia.es* for a free tour. The modest tomb of the world-famous painter Joaquín Sorolla, born in Valencia in 1863, is possibly the most visited. There's usually a red rose left on top.

318 MONOLITH FOR VICTIMS OF THE CIVIL WAR

This sombre monument is dedicated to victims of the Civil War, where they found mass graves of those who were killed by the Franco regime. On the side is a fragment of the poem *El Herido*, by Miguel Hernández, a poet who joined the Quinto Regimiento to fight Franco.

319 SARCÓFAGO DE VICENTE BLASCO IBÁÑEZ

Valencian journalist, politician and novelist Vicente Blasco Ibáñez can also be found resting here. Some of his books were made into Hollywood films, such as *The Four Horsemen of the Apocalypse*. The tombstone reads "...I want my body to be confused with this land of Valencia which is the love of all my loves".

320 GOLD HEADSTONES IN THE CEMETERY CHURCH

There's a church in the centre of the cemetery which holds a peaceful silence. Peep through the glass door to the municipal mausoleum to see 45 notable councillors and governors who, according to the cemetery, gave so much to Valencia that they deserved to have their names immortalised in gold.

The top 5
CABANYAL *capers*

---

321 PARROQUIA DE NUESTRA SEÑORA DE LA BUENA GUÍA

C/ d'Eugènia
Viñes 235
Poblats Maritims ⑧
+34 963 71 19 50

For centuries fishermen in Cabanyal had a church dedicated to Nuestra Señora de la Buena Guía where they prayed for a safe journey before setting sail. The old church was demolished, so in 1958 father Vicente Castelló Palanca founded another. Don't expect grandeur, but the statue of *la virgen* in her boat is charming.

322 LA FÁBRICA DE HIELO

C/ José Ballester
Gozalvo 37
Poblats Maritims ⑧
+34 963 68 26 19
lafabricadehielo.net

Years ago, fish landed in Cabanyal would have been put on ice from this old warehouse. Now it's just as cool, reimagined as a bar with a long terrace just metres from the sand. By day, beachgoers sip beers and at night an eclectic crowd listen to DJs under the corrugated iron roof.

323 SURF LAS ARENAS

C/ de Pavia 85
Poblats Maritims ⑧
+34 678 71 81 71
surflasarenas
valencia.com

Paddling is good, but surfing is better. Surf Las Arenas is a blue-fronted beachy hang-out where friendly instructors teach people of all ages how to shred. Look out for collaborations with other surf camps around Spain for dreamy surfing weekends in rural villas by the sea.

324 MUSEO DEL ARROZ

C/ del Rosari 3
Poblats Maritims ⑧
+34 963 52 54 78
museodelarroz
devalencia.com

The humble grain of rice is crammed full of culture and history. Find out who planted the first fields in the Albufera and admire the engineering of the old machines which whizz and clunk and smell like oil, all housed in a 19th-century mill. You won't look at paella the same way again.

325 MIRADOR DEL PUERTO

AT: MARINA REAL JUAN CARLOS I
Poblats Maritims ⑧

Often overlooked in favour of the beach, the port is a peaceful place for a sunset stroll. Head to Mirador del Puerto, an observation deck with views that reach from the industrial harbour to the beach to the restless blue ocean. Listen to yachts clinking gently in the swell and breathe in fresh salty air.

The 5 greatest
OPEN-AIR EVENTS

---

326 CONCERTS DE VIVERS

AT: JARDINS DE VIVERS
C/ de Cavanilles
La Saïdia ⑥
concertsdevivers.com

The beautifully preened Jardins de Vivers is a whimsical setting for gigs under the stars. Every summer Concerts de Vivers curates a fun line-up, from Cat Power to Italian reggae to local cover bands. Peckish? Graze on hot dogs and pizza from the food trucks on the leafy terrace.

328 LA PÉRGOLA DE LA MARINA

327 FERIA DEL VINO BY MOSTRA PROAVA

AT: JARDÍ DEL TÚRIA
El Pla del Real ⑥
+34 963 92 44 63
proava.org

Taste your way through 150 wines over five days at this relaxed wine fair in the Túria park. Local winemakers chatter and serve generous glasses to visitors under the shade of the rubber trees. 18 breweries cater for grape-averse folks, and a kids play area (with the odd workshop) keeps little people busy.

328 LA PÉRGOLA DE LA MARINA

AT: LA MARINA
Poblats Maritims ⑧
lamarinadevalencia.com

Music fans head to this pretty waterside pergola to tap their toes to bands on sunny Saturday mornings. Concerts take place from around February to early June, and have included day parties by cult record shop Discos Oldies, Spanish shoegaze by Christina Rosenvinge, and glitchy flamenco-punk by Pony Bravo.

329 FERIA DEL CAVA VALENCIANO

AT: MERCAT DE COLÓN
C/ de Jorge Juan
L'Eixample ③
mercadocolon.es

For three days in November, Mercat Colón turns into a temple of cava. The producers are all from Requena: find complex 36-month-aged fizz by Covinas and sparkling pinot noir by Hispano Suizas. Crowds wrap up warm and toast under the warm lights of the Christmas tree.

330 TASTARRÒS

Plaça de
l'Ajuntament
Ciutat Vella ②
arrozdevalencia.org

How do you kick off a rice festival? Throw 10.000 kg of the stuff on the floor, of course. This two-day event invites everyone to use traditional tools to dry the rice mountain, while chefs compete for prizes, bands play out and paellas the size of boats rock up to Plaça de l'Ajuntament.

5 legendary
RUSSAFA institutions

331 UBIK CAFÉ

C/ del Literat
Azorín 13
L'Eixample ③
+34 963 74 12 55
ubikcafe.blogspot.com

Half bookshop half cafe, Ubik is a higgledy-piggledy space where literature, food and art give each other a big fuzzy hug. Browse shelves filled with feminist non-fiction, secondhand Borges and graphic novels before settling at a wonky wooden table for homemade *orecchiette* and a toasty glass of rioja.

332 MADAME MIM

C/ de Puerto Rico 30
L'Eixample ③
+34 963 25 59 41

There are lots of vintage shops in Russafa, but Maria's is the best (and the weirdest). Her self-described freak shop has enough oddities to stock a museum – she's spent years tracking some of them down. Sift through rare Chinese erotic art, snakeskin bags and gigantic poofy tutus.

333 LA BELLA DE CADIZ

C/ de Cadis 54
L'Eixample ③
+34 651 74 57 18

At first glance it looks like an antiques market spilling onto the street, but the kooky decoration of La Bella de Cadiz – with its dummies dressed in Venetian masks and vintage baby carriages in the loo – makes more sense after a few cocktails. *Agua de Valencia* is their speciality, and their mango mojito is potent.

334 LA FINESTRA

C/ dels Vivons 16
L'Eixample ③
+34 963 81 89 85
la-finestra-pizza-restaurant.negocio.site

La Finestra (sister site to Festinar) brings this hidden alley to life, lighting it up with bright murals and a busy terrace. Hungry? Order pizza tapas: tell the bar how many and they'll deliver tiny pizzas with surprise toppings. Cheesy broccoli or olive and spinach are good, but burrata is the jackpot.

335 SALA RUSSAFA

C/ de Dénia 55
L'Eixample ③
salarussafa.es
+34 963 10 74 88

Russafa is known for its arty vibe, and Sala Russafa has been a driving force for theatre and music since 2011. Founded by actors with a shared love of the stage, they host everything from heart-racing productions set in refugee camps to adaptations of whimsical children's books like *¿A qué sabe la luna?*

331 UBIK CAFÉ

5 neat ideas for
RAINY DAYS

---

336 MERCADO DE LA IMPRENTA

C/ de la Mascota 17
Extramurs ④
*mercadodela
imprenta.com*

Plans rained off? Hole up in this characterful covered market, with over 20 different restaurants and bars to choose from. Set in a beautiful old printing press, there's everything from vermouth with olives to healthy smoothies to *arroz al horno* (PS: lots of these rainy tips double up for unbearably hot days too).

337 LA BOLERA

Av. de Campanar 126
Campanar ⑤
+34 963 47 10 11
labolera.es

It's not the biggest or the flashiest bowling alley in Valencia, but it is one of the most central. Find lanes to while away rainy days in La Bolera, or pot balls on the billiards instead. Inside there's a cafe stocked up with plenty of *bravas* and beer.

338 MUSEU FALLER

Plaça de Montolivet 4
Quatre Carreres ⑦
+34 962 08 46 25

We know that every *fallas* is burned in the *cremà*, right? Wrong. The very best are saved for this museum. There are over 80 finely crafted sculptures, which give a unique window into the history of the Fallas festival. Design fans will love the vintage promotional posters; the ones from the 1930s are superb.

339 LOST

C/ Dénia 32
L'Eixample ③
+34 960 28 03 85
lostruzafa.com

Forget singing in the rain, here we sing in private, air-conditioned booths. Inspired by the karaoke scene in *Lost in Translation*, this quirky joint delivers cold beers and cocktails to groups of friends while they belt out *My Way*. Choose between the sultry red Scarlet room or the blue and baby pink Bill room.

340 EL GARAJE FOODIE

C/ del Doctor
Ferran 10
El Pla del Real ⑥
+34 603 01 16 02
elgarajefoodie.com

This 1960s mechanics shop has been dusted off and reinvented as a street food arcade. Inside, a classic car makes a quirky dining table while vintage campervans are converted into food trucks; they're going for the Americana spit 'n' sawdust appearance. Order vegan hot dogs, XL burgers and fried chicken waffles.

5 incredibly
COLOURFUL STREETS

---

341 CARRER DE LA REINA
Poblats Maritims ⑧

A waltz down Cabanyal's Carrer de la Reina reveals rows of old fisherman's houses plastered in colourful tiles, from squares laid like a chessboard to chintzy florals to trippy geometric patterns. Not only did tiles let owners show their personalities, they also help protect buildings from the salty sea air.

342 CARRER DE MORET
Ciutat Vella ①

Carrer de Moret earned the nickname Calle de los Colores for its eye-catching artwork, a project by Alfonso Calza, who owns a photography studio on the road. Local artists united to splash colour on the walls: Luis Lonjedo painted a couple locked in a passionate kiss, and the woman on a bridge is by Deih.

343 CARRER DE BAIX
Ciutat Vella ①

There's a lively energy on this street, perhaps it's down to the vintage shops and jazz bars, or perhaps it's down to the dynamic street art. Walls are covered in mythical, tribal designs by Disneylexya (they're inspired by the Chilean murals of the 1970s) and David de Limón's lovable comic book characters.

344 CARRER DEL ROSARI
Poblats Maritims ⑧

Carrer del Rosari is choc-a-block with colourful street art and ornate houses with wild tiles and plants cascading over wrought iron. Mosey past sunshine-yellow pads, through the palm trees of Plaça del Rosari, before stopping at the tucked away terrace of Bar Lapaca for a vermouth.

345 CARRER DE CUBA – CARRER DE PUERTO RICO
L'Eixample ③

Russafa's streets are generally more colourful than a painter's palette, but the square where Carrer de Cuba and Carrer de Puerto Rico meet is one of the most brilliant. The tropical plants and the retro signage is best enjoyed with a negroni on the terrace of La Flaca.

5 lovely
WALKS

---

346 RUTA DE ARTE
AT: LA MARINA
Poblats Maritims ⑧
lamarinade
valencia.com

Explore the historic port of Valencia through this ready-made street art route, mapped out by La Marina on their website. Follow the coastline and walk along peaceful ports to find 10 urban canvases, from the glitchy, futuristic mural by Argentinian-Spanish artist Felipe Pantone to the joyful, bright smileys of 'I am Laia'.

347 TÚRIA NORTHWEST: TORRES DELS SERRANS TO PARC DE CAPÇALERA
parcdelturia.es

This walk along the old riverbed of the Túria starts at Torres dels Serrans, but join anywhere from the city centre. Stop at El Mas dels Jardiners for a *bocadillo*, and power through to the 330.000-square-metre park, where families cavort in pedalos and wooden walkways offer stunning viewpoints.

348 JARDÍ BOTÀNIC

C/ de Quart 80
Extramurs ④
+34 963 15 68 00
jardibotanic.org

This is a walk for people who don't do walks (and when the sun is beating down, we can all relate). The university took over this abandoned botanical garden in 1987 and transformed it into a lush place to potter. Take a leisurely lap of 4500 different species, from tropical to carnivorous plants.

349 MALVARROSA BEACH TO PATACONA BEACH

The wide walkway on Malvarrosa is an irresistible spot for a sunset promenade. Start at La Fabrica de Hielo with a livener and set off with the sea air behind you. Pass by sunbathers, volleyball players and *cervecerías*, on to Mirador de Patacona for a line-up of brilliant bars and restaurants overlooking the ocean.

350 BOTÀNIC DE L'ALBUFERA

albufera.valencia.es

This peaceful 45-minute route takes in the diverse botany of the dunes in the Albufera. Download the guide and start at Plà de Na Sanxa, named after a woman who grazed her cattle here. Spot the heather and sea grapes in the sand, and breathe deeply from air sweetly scented by rosemary and honeysuckle.

348 **JARDÍ BOTÀNIC**

BOMBAS GENS

50 PLACES TO ENJOY CULTURE

5 intriguing
SMALL MUSEUMS

---

351 **L'IBER – MUSEO DE LOS SOLDADITOS DE PLOMO**
C/ dels Cavallers 20
Ciutat Vella ①
+34 963 91 86 75
museoliber.org

Is any trip to Valencia complete without seeing the world's largest collection of lead soldiers? Absolutely not. A beautifully preserved Gothic mansion is home to these teeny figurines, over 95.000 of them. Collector Álvaro Noguera Giménez meticulously recreated battlefields and local festivals on a miniature scale.

352 **REFUGIO ANTIAÉREO CALLE SERRANOS**
C/ dels Serrans 25
Ciutat Vella ①
+34 604 04 01 50

Valencia was bombed heavily during the Spanish Civil War, and *refugios* like this have been preserved as a reminder of the tragic conflict. Around 400 people would have crammed into this bunker when the air raid sirens went off – there are still doodles of tanks by children on the walls. Book via Whatsapp.

353 **L'ETNO**
C/ de la Corona 36
Ciutat Vella ①
+34 963 88 36 14
letno.dival.es

Also known as the Museu Valencià d'Etnologia, this museum was founded in 1982 to study Valencian culture. Exhibitions are insightful and poignant, like *Les Fosses del Franquisme* (the graves of Francoism), which explores the untold stories of the Spanish Civil War.

354 CASA MUSEO CONCHA PIQUER
C/ de Ruaya 25
La Saïdia ⑥
+34 963 48 56 58

From humble beginnings, Concha Piquer achieved astronomical success. She travelled America, starred in films, and was considered a master of the *copla*. Her birthplace has been turned into a charming museum and features her iconic tour suitcases that she filled with – among other things – olive oil.

355 CASA DE LES ROQUES
C/ de les Roques 1
Ciutat Vella ①
+34 963 15 31 56

An enormous tortoise that seems to float, dragons with teeth the size of bread knives and eagles carved from wood: there's an impressive line-up wheeled out for Corpus Christi, a religious celebration 60 days after Easter. Get to know the animals – and the religious meanings behind them – in this free museum.

355 CASA DE LES ROQUES

356 MUSEU DE BELLES ARTS DE VALÈNCIA

The 5 best museums for

ANCIENT HISTORY

---

356 MUSEU DE BELLES ARTS DE VALÈNCIA

C/ de Sant Pius V 9
La Saïdia ⑥
+34 963 87 03 00
*museobellasartes
valencia.gva.es*

In the second largest art gallery in Spain, grand Gothic rooms present works from the 15th to the 19th centuries. Get close enough to see the craquelure of gilded religious art from the 1400s, and visit the room dedicated to Sorolla where paintings seem to radiate that golden Valencian sun.

357 MUSEU DE L'ALMOINA

Plaça de Dècim
Juni Brut
Ciutat Vella ①
+34 962 08 41 73

Found in a quiet square behind the cathedral, this subterranean museum is a gift for those who want to learn about the roots of Valencia. Head downstairs and walk through a hidden network of streets dating back to the Roman and Moorish era, the original footpaths of the ancient city. Free entry on Sundays.

358 CRIPTA DE LA CÁRCEL DE SAN VICENTE MÁRTIR

Plaça de l'Arquebisbe 3
Ciutat Vella ①
+34 962 08 45 73

This little-known relic was a funeral chapel linked to the cathedral, and holds the remains of a Valencian Bishop. Inside the dark and musty room it's usually empty, the deathly silence broken only by haunting music. Approach the bishop's bones and get goose bumps; with the place to yourself it's genuinely moving.

359 MUSEU DE PREHISTÒRIA DE VALÈNCIA

AT: L'ETNO
C/ de la Corona 36
Ciutat Vella ①
+34 963 88 35 65
mupreva.org

Found within the bigger L'ETNO museum, this huge exhibition is a properly jaw-dropping collection of bones, artefacts and pots, dating from the Lower Paleolithic Age to the Romans. Discover barnacle-covered amphoras and human skulls that bear the bite marks of big cats, all found within the Valencian community.

360 MUSEO DE CIENCIAS NATURALES

AT: JARDINS DE VIVERS
C/ del General Elio
La Saïdia ⑥
+34 962 08 43 13

Dinosaurs hide amongst the flowerbeds of Jardins de Vivers – contained within this museum, of course. Valencian Rodrigo Botet was exiled for being a *Carlista* and reinvented himself as an engineer in Buenos Aires. He made a fortune and gifted this collection to Valencia – a novel way to get back in the city's good books.

5 brilliant
THEATRES *and* STAGES

361 **TEATRE TALIA**
C/ dels Cavallers 31
Ciutat Vella ①
+34 963 91 29 20
teatretalia.es

Teatre Talia is a vision in red. The seats, stage and that heavy gold-fringed curtain are all classic tomato-red, with glitzy details. It was founded in 1928 to appeal to people of all walks of life. Today it hosts drama, flamenco and comedy to appeal to a wide audience – so no snooty thespians here.

362 **TEATRO OLYMPIA**
C/ de Sant Vicent
Màrtir 44
Ciutat Vella ②
+34 963 51 73 15
teatro-olympia.com

Even the lobby of Teatro Olympia, with its stained glass ceiling and Greek columns, is glamorous. It's been operating as a theatre since 1915 and was declared a historical site in 2021. Overlooking the stage, intricately sculpted boxes are highlighted in gold, and velvet red seats take in everything from musicals to ballet.

363 CAFÉ DEL DUENDE

C/ del Túria 62
Extramurs ①
+34 630 45 52 89
cafedelduende.com

This tiny flamenco den fills up quickly – arrive in good time and find a candlelit table close enough to feel a whoosh of air as the ruffled skirts twirl. People flock here for fierce dancing and soulful singing. They come to experience *duende*, the Spanish word for the deep emotions stirred by flamenco.

364 ESPACIO INESTABLE

C/ d'Aparisi i
Guijarro 7
Ciutat Vella ①
+34 963 91 95 50
espacioinestable.com

This intimate venue hosts offbeat performances with a view to support modern theatre and dance. Visit for surreal dramas like *Moscas Aplastadas* by Carla Zúñiga, which explores maternity through open-ended metaphors, or an intense workshop on the language of improvisation and expression by Alba Vayá.

365 SALA ULTRAMAR

C/ d'Alzira 9
Extramurs ④
+34 962 06 26 98
salaultramar.com

Those seeking the bravest and most daring productions know to venture into Sala Ultramar, a space where seats are so close to the stage that the audience feels like part of the set. Don't speak Valencian? Try the dance-meets-acrobatics show *Otempodiz*, a spellbinding exchange between Mozambique and Spain.

5 FESTIVALS
you need to know about

—————————

366 FALLAS
MARCH 15-19

Wild, noisy and fuelled by fire, this festival dedicated to Saint Joseph gets its name from the enormous wooden sculptures which pop up in the *plaças*. Admire the handiwork and social commentary before they're burnt to a crisp in the *cremà*. Party on the streets, eating *buñuelos* and dodging *petardos*, from March 15-19.

367 CORPUS CHRISTI
60 DAYS AFTER EASTER

The colourful religious event dates back to 1355. It takes place 60 days after Easter; the church bells peal while red and white petals rain from the balconies. They fall on parading characters: giant puppets whirl down the streets and local dance troupes act out the triumph of good over evil to the sound of the *dolçaina*.

368 FESTA DE LA MARE DE DÉU DELS DESAMPARATS

2ND SUNDAY OF MAY

On the second Sunday of May Valencia celebrates their much-loved patron saint *La Mare de Déu dels Desamparats*, or *Virgen de los Desamparados* in Castellano. There's a busy schedule: dances, open-air theatre, and the procession of the patron saint herself (it takes around 120 people to carry her, in groups of 32).

369 FESTIVIDAD DE SAN ANTONIO ABAD

JANUARY 17
AT: PARROQUIA SAN ANTONIO ABAD
C/ de Sagunt 188
La Saïdia ⑥

On January 17 thousands of creatures, from cats and dogs to tortoises and chameleons, gather at San Antonio Abad Church. It started in the 18th century, when peasants would take their horses to a church in La Saïdia, where it was said a branch from the church's olive tree would give animals good health.

370 NOU D'OCTUBRE

OCTOBER 9
Plaça d'Alfons
el Magnànim
Ciutat Vella
and all across
the city

In 1238 King Jaime I completed his conquest of Valencia, and on October 9 he kissed the ground of his new city. To commemorate, the Senyera flag is taken to the King's statue and surrounded by a sea of flowers. Look out for little marzipan fruit and veggies (*mocadoràs*) – men traditionally give them to their sweethearts.

5 venues for
UP-AND-COMING
BANDS

---

371 LOCO CLUB

**Carrer de l'Erudit
Orellana 12
Extramurs ④
+34 963 51 85 21**
lococlub.es

Under the spinning disco ball music-lovers bop to psychedelic cumbia by Xixa Morá, groove to funk and soul outfit Ay Trick, and sing along to catchy punk-pop by Lisasinson. Loco Club packs a punch for such a small venue, and on Friday and Saturday nights DJs spin records after the bands.

372 KAF CAFÉ

**Plaça d'Emili Beüt
i Belenguer 7
Benimaclet ⑥
+34 663 70 29 60**
kafcafe.eatbu.com

Community-driven Kaf Café has a hotchpotch interior with its wall mounted bicycle, chunky pebbledash bar, and Tetris-stacked bookshelves. The poetry slam is most well known, but the low-fi gigs (expect acoustic folk and gypsy jazz) are equally good. A no-frills menu offers *empanadas*, burgers and *patatas bravas* to nibble on.

373 BLACK NOTE CLUB

C/ de Polo y
Peyrolón 15
El Pla del Real ⑥
+34 619 39 46 65
blacknoteclub.com

Black Note Club is a great little venue to bop around to rock, indie and soul. Established in 1993, it hosts everything from swing jazz to Queen cover bands to hardcore punk. Want your five minutes of fame? The Wednesday jam session invites anyone who can play an instrument up on stage.

374 LA CASA DE LA MAR

Av. Vicent Blasco
Ibañez 8
Alboraia ⑧
+34 627 23 24 46
lacasadelamar.com

Near Patacona beach, an old shipbuilding warehouse has been transformed with beer, bands and plywood. Friends gather on long communal benches while kids play on tables made from wooden pallets. Soulful Argentinian folk band Fémina have graced the stage, as have the glitchy new wave trio Amor Butano.

375 CENTRO EXCURSIONISTA

C/ Marqués de
Zenete 4
Extramurs ④
+34 960 82 53 20

Musician Xema Fuertes toured the world and made a mental note of the best bars he found. He combined his favourite elements in this fantastic dive bar: the popcorn machine, the antique mirrors, the low lighting. It's a goldmine for music fans. On Wednesday they pit Roomba vacuums against each other – it's wild.

The 5 best
JAZZ BARS

---

376 MATISSE CLUB

C/ de Campoamor 60
Algirós ⑦
+34 685 24 00 14
matisseclub.com

Valencia has had a long love affair with jazz, and Berklee's local campus has a big part to play in it. Every Thursday a group of Berklee students called Sala E lead a jam at Matisse Club, and the 5-euro ticket includes a drink. The venue also hosts rising local stars, with a focus on classical, jazz, afrobeat and hip-hop.

377 LA VITTI

Plaça del Xúquer 3
Algirós ⑦
+34 963 38 91 51

La Vitti has gained a loyal following for its living room-style gigs. Arrive early for the sofas or perch on a bookshelf. Folks often sit on the floor to glimpse the lead singer scatting or the cellist's solo. The band play on a stage so small that they can't all fit, with a backdrop of fairy lights and Tiffany lamps.

378 JIMMY GLASS

C/ de Baix 28
Ciutat Vella ①
+34 656 89 01 43
jimmyglassjazz.net

Jimmy Glass has been seeking out and supporting new talent in the jazz scene since the 1990s. Find everything from Basel-based Yumi Ito and her ethereal art-pop to Azerbaijan-based pianist and composer Amina Figarova. It's a serious hang-out for jazz lovers, but it's not too stuffy.

379 MARINO JAZZ BAR

C/ d'Eugènia
Viñes 223
Poblats Maritims ⑧
marinojazz.com

Leave the bright seafront and slip into Marino Jazz Bar for a well-made cocktail and a dimly-lit table. Here they don't want to push boundaries, it's more about the classics and the sultry vibe than experimental solos. Thursday is jazz night, with live performances followed by a freewheeling jam.

380 CAFÉ MERCEDES JAZZ

C/ de Sueca 27
L'Eixample ③
+34 602 60 07 53
cafemercedes.es

It's only been open since 2007 but Café Mercedes Jazz has made a name for itself with international acts and local talent. The Russafa hang-out was founded in honour of Mercedes Rossy, a talented pianist who passed away aged 34, and they bolster the music scene through cultural and artistic exchanges in her memory.

5 charming independent
CINEMAS

381 LA FILMOTECA
**Plaça de
l'Ajuntament 17
Ciutat Vella** ②
+34 962 93 66 21
ivc.gva.es

La Filmoteca was founded in 1985 to preserve Valencian cinema, and in 1988 it made the historic Rialto building their home (they've since stashed over 35.000 titles in their archives). The festival Filmoteca D'Estiu collates the most decorated films and shows them at Rialto and their open-air screen by Palau de la Musica.

382 EL MAR QUE NOS MIRA

AT: LA RAMBLETA
C/ de Pius IX 2
Jesús ④
larambleta.com

Sweltering evenings in July and August are a little cooler thanks to this cinema under the stars. El Mar Que Nos Mira is a seasonal movie house set up by La Rambleta on their terrace with a soft focus on Mediterranean films. Watch nail-biting dramas and Spanish black comedy while scoffing popcorn.

383 CINEMA JOVE

Various locations
cinemajove.com

Every June, Cinema Jove floods the city with brilliant international flicks and opportunities for young filmmakers to flex. Find competitions for directors aged 5 to 25 years old, screenings of very early releases by iconic names like the Coen Brothers, and screenings at cool, unexpected venues around the city.

384 CINES BABEL

C/ de Vicent Sancho
Tello 10
El Pla del Real ⑥
+34 963 62 67 95
cinesalbatrosbabel.com

One of the most charming cinemas in Valencia, Cines Babel offers five small screens, nostalgic card tickets on entry and vintage film posters in the adjoining restaurant. It also shows films in the original language, never dubbed, which means that the subtleties of Tom Hanks' delivery in Asteroid City are not lost in translation.

385 CINESTUDIO D'OR

C/ de l'Almirall
Cadarso 31
L'Eixample ③
cinestudiodor.es

Founded in 1951, this is the oldest cinema in Valencia and interiors retain that mid-century magic. Fancy a film marathon? One ticket is valid for two films. Brush up on your Spanish though, all the movies are dubbed in Castellano.

5 essential

MODERN ART

galleries

---

386 INSTITUTO VALENCIANO DE ARTE MODERNO

C/ de Guillem de Castro 118
Ciutat Vella ①
+34 963 17 66 00
ivam.es

IVAM should be the first port of call for modern art fans. The large building is home to a huge selection of Spanish, European and American work, which spans constructivism, Dadaism and futurism to contemporary conceptual art by the likes of Gillian Wearing and political sculpture by Mona Hatoum.

387 CENTRE DEL CARME DE CULTURA CONTEMPORÀNIA

C/ del Museu 2
Ciutat Vella ①
+34 963 15 20 24
consorcimuseus.gva.es

Art, film and music are neatly bundled into one incredible building at CCCC. Exhibits are interactive and accessible, shining a light on local current affairs. The 13th-century monastery is stunning – it's easy to imagine monks pottering in the calm leafy courtyard. Use it as an escape from El Carmen's busy streets.

388 VANGAR

C/ de Pere III el Gran 22
L'Eixample ③
+34 962 02 42 00
galeriavangar.com

This gallery is based in a beautiful old building dating back to 1935, reimagined as a minimal hide-out for modern art. Their raison d'être is to boost the work of emerging artists; see fresh talent from the local university, like the experimental graphics of Alba Abellán.

389 BOMBAS GENS

Av. de Burjassot 54
La Saïdia ⑥
+34 963 46 38 56
bombasgens.com

A 1930s mechanic's shop, surrounded by high-rise flats and sleepy bars, is the unlikely location of one of Valencia's most dynamic galleries. A cool crowd gathers for events, like boundaryless ballet where dancers spin through the galleries. The garden, with its pomegranate trees and glass baubles, is especially beautiful.

390 GALERÍA THEMA

C/ Ciril Amorós 87
L'Eixample ③
+34 963 33 93 61
galeriathema.com

Classic and understated, Galería Thema supplies collectors and day trippers alike with contemporary art. Find signed lithographs by Joan Miró, drawings of naked folks by Pablo Picasso and pop art by Manolo Valdés. Exhibitions focus on local talent, like the looping metallic sculptures of Rafael Amorós.

389 **BOMBAS GENS**

5 offbeat
ALTERNATIVE ART
galleries

391 **SPORTING CLUB RUSSAFA**
C/ de Sevilla 5
L'Eixample ③
+34 606 22 28 78
sportingclub russafa.com

By no means reserved for the local artistic milieu, visitors are welcomed with open arms to Sporting Club Russafa and given impromptu tours of the paint-splattered workshops. Inside, cluttered artists' studios and a stage dedicated to book launches and lectures huddle under a vast old warehouse roof.

392 **HOUSE OF CHAPPAZ**
C/ dels Cavallers 35
Ciutat Vella ①
+34 696 19 02 85
houseofchappaz.com

Aptly nicknamed 'the flat', entry to this miniscule space requires a leap of faith. Find the residential block and ring the unmarked doorbell to discover a spaceship-like room of cutting-edge art. Sound intimidating? Far from it. Staff are warm and welcoming – it's a second home for the underground arts scene. Booking essential.

393 TUESDAY TO FRIDAY

C/ Sant Pere
Pasqual 7
Extramurs ④
+34 963 36 31 32
tuesdaytofriday.com

Up-and-coming artists are given a space to shine in Tuesday to Friday, a compact gallery that explores the digital age and society. The show *Summer Mix Vol. 1* asked artists to create something inspired by an old summer anthem. The result was a bright, nostalgic exhibition, with a terrific playlist to match.

①

394 LUIS ADELANTADO

C/ de Bonaire 6
Ciutat Vella ②
+34 963 51 01 79
luisadelantadovlc.com

Olga Adelantado runs this pin-sharp gallery, while her father Luis spearheads the sister site in Mexico. The Valencia project introduces quality, exciting work, like the Parisian couple and creative duo Lamarche-Ovize who make lamps with ceramic tentacles and paintings of fantasy gardens with a nod to Arts and Crafts.

395 GABINETE DE DIBUJOS

C/ del Literat
Azorín 33
L'Eixample ③
+34 963 42 06 79
gabinetededibujos.com

Founded in 2020, this stylish space is found in an old garage in Russafa. It's dedicated to contemporary drawings, but looks at the theme through a wide lens. Think abstract yet hyper-realistic botanical sketches, letters in hundreds of different fonts, or abstract lines trying to capture a childlike innocence.

394 **LUIS ADELANTADO**

5 examples of iconic
STREET ART

**396 MAI S'APAGARÀ
LA NOSTRA LLUM**
BY BARBITURIKILLS
C/ del Progrés 183
Poblats Maritims ⑧
+34 620 68 45 52
barbiturikills.com

Bárbara Sebastián is a Valencian street artist known for her joyful pink rabbits, which always deliver a serious message. This work is a homage to the strength of Cabanyal residents, who successfully blocked a plan by the local council to bulldoze part of the historic neighbourhood. Google 'Salvem el Cabanyal' for more background.

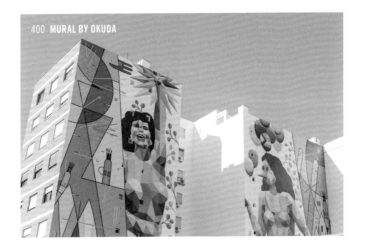
400 MURAL BY OKUDA

397 MURAL

BY CABISCOL

C/ de Pintor Fillol /
C/ Roteros
Ciutat Vella ①

Cabiscol has covered every inch of an old office in a dreamlike mural of cacti, cave houses, geometric prints and someone riding a rhinoceros. What's it about? Perhaps it's an imagined prehistoric scene in Valencia, perhaps it's a social commentary on how people live in Valencia today. Whatever it is, it's impressive.

398 DISSENY MADE IN COOP

BY CACHETEJACK

C/ de la
Beneficència 16
Ciutat Vella ①

Cachetejack is the name of illustrator duo Nuria Bellver and Raquel Fanjul, who make the most vibrant street art. This mural is especially happy and energetic; the image of three people working together talks about the power of cooperation – as is the fact that these two have collaborated since they met at university.

399 LOOK INSIDE

BY CACHETEJACK

Gran Via de Ferran
el Catòlic 67
Extramurs ④
cachetejack.com

On the Gran Via, a hot pink building pops against the blue sky. A 600-square-metre head seems to be looking inwards. Chunky lettering reads: 'LOOK INSIDE'. It's another masterpiece by Cachetejack, a mural that asks people to reflect, be calm, and empathise in a time of polarisation.

400 MURAL

BY OKUDA
AT: JOAQUÍN
SOROLLA STATION
Extramurs ④

Oscar San Miguel Erice, also known as Okuda, is a Spanish artist with incredible vision. His vivid, geometric murals search for the joy in life's darkest avenues. This mural celebrates diversity, community and being outdoors – it was completed just a year after Spain's lockdown.

PARC GULLIVER

20 THINGS TO DO WITH CHILDREN

5 RESTAURANTS WITH PARKS *outside*

401 IO RESTAURANTE

C/ de Dalt 30
Ciutat Vella ①
+34 963 15 52 26
iorestaurante.com

Sheltered in a little square and shaded by a gigantic old rubber tree, this restaurant has an enclosed play area (aimed at older children, but with plenty of room for toddlers to toddle), colouring sheets and crayons, and brilliant tapas. Order nachos and slow-cooked parmigiana that's so good the family will fight over it.

402 LE FAVOLE

C/ de l'Hedra 5
Ciutat Vella ②
+34 961 67 26 30
lefavole.es

With its fancy fit-out and large terrace, this Italian restaurant is popular with families for special occasions. Book a terrace table to be close to the children's playground. Watch your little ones play on the slides and swings while dining on hearty bowls of pasta with generous glasses of Nero d'Avola.

403 CAFÉ LA PLACITA

Plaça San Sebastián 9
Extramurs ④
+34 697 81 97 12
cafelaplacita.com

Kids or no kids, this tapas bar in a sunny square is totally idyllic. It's not a big play area (spring horses, a seesaw and no fence), but there is space for children to roam. It serves classics done well, like *huevos rotos* with *bravas* and runny yolks, and Valencian tomatoes topped with burrata.

404 LA MALCRIADA

C/ de l'Actor
Rivelles 5
Ciutat Vella ②
+34 640 34 91 66
*lamalcriada
gastrobar.com*

This recently revamped playground – complete with climbing frame, swing and monkey bars – is close to Mercat Central, making it a great spot for a post-market picnic. Otherwise, La Malcriada bar has an affordable two-course lunch deal. It might include *bravas* with oodles of *aioli*, or *arroz del senyoret*.

405 ORXATERIA VIDA

Partida de Saboia 6
Alboraia
+34 622 66 98 64

It's a 20-minute bike ride to this peaceful farmhouse, where children can meet peacocks, play in the grass and scale the climbing wall before cooling off with a freshly squeezed orange juice. Owners Vicente and Vicenta make *horchata* using their own tiger nuts and squidgy cake using pumpkins from their farm.

5 magical
INDOOR PLAY AREAS

---

406 ANTIGUO ALMACÉN DE DIENTES

C/ de Borrull 16
Extramurs ④
+34 640 67 97 93
*antiguoalmacen
dedientes.com*

Lost a tooth? Friendly mouse Ratoncito Pérez is responsible for retrieving it and leaving a present. This is his HQ. An interactive factory managed by two human theatre-lovers who wanted to create a space for children's imaginations to run wild. Kids will love spotting the mini train and peeking inside the tooth factory.

407 SMILELAND

Av. de Catalunya 8
El Pla del Real ⑥
smilelandclub.es

There's a genuinely nice atmosphere in this pastel-coloured playpark. On one side of the white picket fence parents drink *cafe con leche*, and on the other children explore pink child-sized mansions, whizz about on classic cars and surf on wooden balance boards while staff cheer them on.

408 ESPAI DE TELLES

AT: CENTRE DEL
CARME DE CULTURA
CONTEMPORÀNIA
C/ del Museu 2
Ciutat Vella ①
+34 963 15 20 24
consorcimuseus.gva.es

Email ahead and this room in CCCC will be all yours for free. Aimed at 0-to-3-year olds, the big pea-green playroom is designed for unstructured free play and features cushions, mirrors, dreamy music and a wonky terrain. Big lights in the floor are inspired by the 'tavolo luminoso Montessori' used in Reggio Emilia.

409 TEATRO LA ESTRELLA

C/ dels Àngels 33
Poblats Marítims ⑧
+34 963 56 22 92
teatrolaestrella.com

Founded in 1995 in an old Cabanyal manor house, this puppet theatre is unbelievably cute: frontage is sky-blue with hand-painted tiles, and corridors have become a museum of characters from previous productions. Watch plays like *El Patito Feo* performed with handmade string puppets. Parents and children will be smitten.

410 HEMISFÈRIC

Av. del Professor
López Piñero 3
Quatre Carreres ⑦
+34 961 97 46 86
cac.es/hemisferic

Designed by Santiago Calatrava, this spherical cinema is the largest in Spain: a concave screen over 900 square metres. It was designed to resemble an eye, a nod to the observation and learning that takes place inside. Films include *Oceans. Our Blue Planet*, which teaches viewers about mysterious sea creatures.

408 ESPAI DE TELLES

5 **PARKS** and **PLAYGROUNDS**

for little explorers

411 **PARC GULLIVER**

AT: JARDÍ DEL TÚRIA
**Near Pont de
l'Àngel Custodi
El Pla del Real** ⑦
+34 963 37 02 04
*parcdelturia.es/
actividades/parque-
gulliver*

Entertaining little people since 1990, Gulliver Park is an enormous interactive sculpture of Jonathan Swift's Gulliver sprawled on the floor. It depicts the moment when the explorer arrives in Lilliput and the tiny inhabitants restrain him. The park is wildly popular, with Lilliputians sliding down hair and jumping over fingers.

411 PARC GULLIVER

412 PATACONA BEACH PLAYGROUND

Passeig Marítim de la Patacona, Opposite Casa Navarro
Alboraia ⑧

There are lots of parks along the seafront, but this one in Patacona with its feet in the sand is especially picturesque. Parents are treated to ocean views while children zoom down slides and walk over wobbly bridges. Pop in to the nearby *chiringuito* (only open in summer) to pick up a coffee while little folks play.

413 CENTRO FERROVIARIO VAPORISTA DE RIBA-ROJA DE TÚRIA

C/ Ausiàs March 6
Riba-roja de Túria
+34 603 40 25 40
cfvrt.com

An enthusiastic team of volunteers look after the miniature steam train that ferries passengers between ponds, plants and over a little ravine. Picnic tables, cafes and playgrounds complete the package. It's a 30-minute drive from the city and worth every minute. Open Sundays from 11 am – 1.30 pm; the train takes cash only.

414 JARDINS DE VIVERS

C/ de Cavanilles 1
La Saïdia ⑥

In the middle of this historic park, near the entrance opposite Avinguda de Blasco Ibáñez, a large playground is popular with an after-school crowd. Its best feature is a miniature road network, complete with little traffic lights and crossings.

415 PARC DE L'OEST

Av. del Cid 35
Patraix ④

After a major renovation this park is a regular hang-out for locals, especially families. It's built on the former headquarters of the Spanish Air Force – spot the jet that seems to be taking off into the sky. Get stuck into pétanque courts, swings, slides and – when it's really hot – cool off in the swimming pool next door.

The 5 best **TOY SHOPS** and **BABY BOUTIQUES**

---

416 **CECILIA PLAZA**

C/ de Quart 52
Ciutat Vella ①
+34 960 91 17 91
ceciliaplaza.com

Cecilia Plaza is a Valencian illustrator, who applies her craft to lovely keepsakes like cups and saucers, children's growth charts, handmade playmats, and adorable alphabet banners for kid's bedrooms. At Christmas she sells sustainable organic cotton advent calendars with envelopes ready to be filled with little surprises.

417 **BAMBOO KIDS**

C/ del Literat
Azorín 47
L'Eixample ③
+34 662 69 45 53

Not only is Bamboo Kids thoughtfully stocked with sustainable toys, sunglasses, books and barefoot shoes, it has a play area lit by fairy lights where kids can snuggle up on the sofa and flick through fairy tales, play the tiny drum kit or whip up some ice-cream sundaes in the mini kitchen. Pair with a trip to Parc Central opposite.

418 GRANUJAS, CRIANZA SOSTENIBLE

C/ de Calixt III 18
Extramurs ④
+34 960 44 07 85
granujas.es

From cloth nappies to bamboo tooth-brushes to reusable lactation pads, this store stocks things to make parenting as sustainable as possible. They have a huge range of slings – it's their speciality, and some of them are available to rent. Pop in to try on ultra-light summer wraps and flowy organic cotton carriers.

419 BORDADOS GALMAN

Plaça Redona 16
Ciutat Vella ②
+34 81 86 44
bordadosgalman.es

There's nothing cuter than knitted booties, and this long-established shop in the Plaça Redona has a shed load. Their selection of woolly bonnets and cardigans with pom-poms has reduced grown men to tears. Too hot for knitwear? Kit the kids out in frilly bloomers and vichy dresses or adorable poofy rompers.

420 DIDECO

C/ d'Hernán Cortés 17
L'Eixample ③
+34 963 52 21 65
dideco.es

Beware: enter this shop with children and they will attempt to move in and change the locks. The Spanish chain is a treasure chest of toys, fancy dress outfits, books and brightly coloured knick-knacks for ages 0 to 12. Tuesday is grandparents day – show them your grandkids (picture or IRL) to get 10% off.

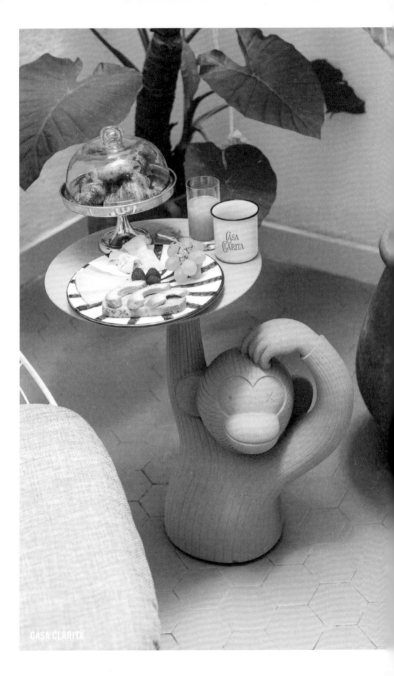

CASA CLARITA

25 PLACES
TO SLEEP

5
COOL and MODERN
hotels

421 CASA CLARITA

C/ de les Avellanes 10
Ciutat Vella ②
+34 963 02 20 60
casaclarita.com

Casa Clarita is what happens when you let a phenomenal artist loose on a hotel. Jaime Hayon uses fun shapes and fresh Mediterranean design – it makes for a brilliant sleepover. Tiles are chequered on the walls, hexagonal flowers on the floor. Spot the blue vases, inspired by the building's previous life as a glass workshop.

421 CASA CLARITA

422 HELEN BERGER

C/ de les Comèdies 24
Ciutat Vella ②
+34 960 47 91 36
hotelhelenberger.com

Helen Berger is a chic hub for exploring the churches and historic streets of La Xerea. All 34 rooms are dressed in cool tones with rich walnut cladding – bag the attic room for a secluded sun terrace with candy-striped sofas. Ask for eggs to be delivered straight to the marshmallow-soft bed in a wicker breakfast tray.

423 COSMO HOTEL AND BAR

Av. de María Cristina 8
Ciutat Vella ②
+34 960 47 93 01
hotelcosmo
valencia.com

Minimal, modern and opposite Mercat Central, Cosmo is a snazzy base for long weekends. Rooms are stripped back but comfortable, and the mustard-yellow restaurant serves food from 7 am until midnight. Find time to try the cocktail menu on the secret rooftop terrace.

424 THE VALENTIA CORRETGERÍA

C/ de la Corretgeria 28
Ciutat Vella ①
+34 960 91 81 97
thevalentia.es

Wake up to terracotta pots of banana plants and fig trees at The Valentia, a divine refuge in the old town with a lush terrace for morning coffee. Launched in 2023, the rooms are sparkling new with gold fittings. Some rooms have wrought iron balconies with views of the winding streets and ornate old houses.

425 REINA 107

C/ de la Reina 107
Poblats Maritims ⑧
+34 679 74 04 21
reina107.es

Don't be fooled by the façade of this 100-year-old building, inside has been smartened up with a contemporary fit-out, with moody shades of black and gray warmed by rattan and velvet furniture. Rooms are small and there's no breakfast option, but roll out of bed and you're practically on the beach.

The 5 best
LUXURIOUS *hotels*

426 CARO HOTEL

C/ de l'Almirall 14
Ciutat Vella ①
+34 963 05 90 00
carohotel.com

When bosses started restoring this old mansion in La Xerea, they didn't know they'd uncover Roman mosaics, old Arab city walls (go see them in the restaurant downstairs), and even the remains of Roman soldiers. History pours from this 26-room luxury hotel, where architecture and understated design blend seamlessly.

426 CARO HOTEL

427 ONLY YOU

Plaça de Rodrigo
Botet 5
Ciutat Vella ②
+34 963 98 10 00
onlyyouhotels.com

Glitzy interiors by Lázaro Rosa-Violán make guests arriving at this five-star hotel feel like they're walking the red carpet. Rooms are elegant, with rolltop baths and some with panoramic views of the city from the bed. The plants flowing from the cocktail bar echo neighbouring balconies, a lovely spot for people watching.

428 THE WESTIN VALENCIA

C/ d'Amadeu de
Savoia 16
El Pla del Real ⑥
+34 963 62 59 00
marriott.com

Open since 2006, The Westin Valencia is an old-timer in the luxury hotel scene. The classic design has aged well, and art deco-style rooms with chandeliers and polished marble feel like stepping back in time. With 135 rooms it is immense, but service is warm and meticulous.

429 HOTEL MARQUÉS HOUSE

C/ de l'Abadia de
Sant Martí 10
Ciutat Vella ②
+34 960 66 05 06
myrhotels.com/hoteles/
hotel-marques-house

With just 29 rooms this hotel feels small and cosy. Decor is eclectic, with wacky parrot wallpaper in the breakfast room and lights hanging from turquoise ropes, but the rooms are more muted. The bar on the ground floor is famous for inventing *Agua de Valencia*; order via room service to enjoy on the terrace.

430 HOTEL PALACIO VALLIER

Plaça de Manises 7
Ciutat Vella ①
+34 960 66 13 06
myrhotels.com

Going all out? This five-star 19th-century mansion takes some beating. From the valet service to the handsome rooftop terrace to the art deco-style rooms, everything is impeccable. A drink in the Lladro Lounge is a must; friendly staff treat guests like VIPs and mix killer cocktails, like a potent Nuclear Daiquiri.

5 hotels
NEAR THE BEACH

431 LA CASA DEL PUERTO

C/ del Pare Lluís
Navarro 3
Poblats Marítims ⑧
+34 963 81 10 00
apartamentos
lamasbonita.es

Not only does La Más Bonita run great cafes, they host a mean holiday rental, too. The hospitality moguls have transformed an old house near the port into four hippie hideaways. Kitchens have Smeg fridges, the gnarled beams are exposed, bedrooms boast boho wicker beds, and free bikes are included.

432 HOTEL BALNEARIO LAS ARENAS

C/ d'Eugènia
Viñes 22
Poblats Marítims ⑧
+34 963 12 06 00
hotelvalencia
lasarenas.com

This enormous five-star hotel looks modern, but it dates back to 1898. It's always been lavish: in the 1920s they would assemble a pier every summer where they would host orchestras and dances. The pier has sadly gone, but sculpted gardens conceal three swimming pools, a spa, and grand rooms with sea views.

433 HOTEL BOUTIQUE BALANDRET

Passeig de Neptú 20
Poblats Maritims ⑧
+34 963 81 11 41
balandret.com

Balandret couldn't get closer to the beach if it tried. Simple rooms are kitted out with all the basics, and if you didn't bag one with a sea view, head upstairs to the terrace. It's a relaxing retreat cooled by the sea breeze, where guests order bottles of Valencian wine with cheese boards while watching the waves roll in.

434 BANANA BEACH

Av. Mare Nostrum 2
Alboraia ⑧
+34 962 14 22 05
bananabeach-
patacona.com

This funky B&B on the cooler end of Valencia's beach has a prime location above the matcha lattes and vitamin-loaded smoothies of Banana Beach restaurant. Double rooms are simple but modern, and the two-bedroom apartment has a large terrace with outdoor seating and views down to the deep blue sea.

435 LÍNDALA

C/ d'Ernest
Anastasio 46
Poblats Maritims ⑧
+34 660 71 36 60
lindalavalencia.com

There is a down-to-earth charm about Líndala, perhaps it's the earthy straw lamps, wooden furniture and the sun-dappled terrace, shaded with bamboo mats and tropical green leaves. Rooms are simple but cosy; a good base to explore the century-old *tabernas* and tiled fishermen's houses nearby.

5 *trailblazing*
S U S T A I N A B L E *hotels*

436 **CASAS BENALI**

C/ de Benalí, km 18
Enguera
+34 628 01 98 72
casasbenali.com

When Daniel and Martine found this tiny hamlet in the mountains, they fell in love with it. They transformed it into a sustainable refuge, a self-contained village of double rooms, rustic houses, tipis and terraces with views of the countryside. Book individual rooms, or recharge the batteries at a wholesome yoga retreat.

437 **YOURS**

C/ de Cuba 19
L'Eixample ③
+34 960 43 93 20
thisisyours.es

Set in an old laundrette in Russafa, everything in this minimal hotel has been meticulously thought through. Owners worked with nearby artisans to bring their vision to life, from hand-poured candles, to cups thrown by a local ceramicist, to coffee roasted by Bluebell just down the road.

438 **MAR DE FULLES**

Polígono 5,
Parcela 69
Alfondeguilla
+34 964 09 09 65
mardefulles.es

Guests at this 100% solar-powered hotel get to fling open the doors to their private terrace and let in the breeze and the birdsong from the Serra d'Espadà mountain range. A 50-minute drive from Valencia, lazy afternoons are spent reading a book by the saltwater swimming pool and sipping organic wine.

439 VILLA SERRANO

C/ Valencia
Pedrones 16
Los Pedrones
+34 620 92 06 33
villaserrano.es

An hour's drive from Valencia, this 1920s home in the quaint village of Los Pedrones was renovated with a very light touch. Hydraulic tiles were preserved, wooden fixtures oiled, and a wood-fired hot tub added. Supporting local businesses are at the heart of their project; hit the high street for a tour of the local winery.

440 CENTRO CALIMA

C/ Nova Malvarrosa 11
Gilet
+34 626 91 78 01
centrocalima.com

Centro Calima is a restorative combination of yoga, meditation, and nutritious cooking by Marta (she works wonders with plant-based ingredients) just a 30-minute drive from the city centre. Safari tents, which cocoon guests in the great outdoors, can be booked individually, but it comes into its own during group retreats.

437 YOURS

5 cosy
SMALL BUDGET *hotels*

---

441 **BALCÓN AL MAR**

C/ de Joan Josep
Sister 1
Poblats Marítims ⑧
+34 963 30 06 38
hostalbalconalmar.es

The interiors aren't anything to write home about, but the snug double rooms with air conditioning and balconies in these Cabanyal digs start from just 50 euro. The hotel also has a little shop where you can buy locally made goodies, like organic honey and Utopick small-batch chocolate bars.

442 **ART & FLATS**

Av. del Oeste 37
Ciutat Vella ②
+34 960 69 71 39
artandflats.com

These budget two-bedroom flats come with pop-art pictures and a communal terrace and dining space. Avunguda del Oeste is one of the busier roads in the city, but for friends who want to be slap bang in the middle of it, it's a winner. Apartments start from around 85 euro a night, with a two night minimum.

443 THE VENUE HOSTEL

C/ de Dolores
Alcaide 14
Jesús ④
+34 662 11 80 51
thevenuehostel.com

From summer beer pong tournaments with a 200-euro prize pot to workspaces dedicated to digital nomads, this *hostal* works hard to suit every type of visitor. Choose between big double rooms with separate living spaces for 126 euro or mixed 10-bed dorms with individual lockers for 30 euro a night.

444 THE RIVER HOSTEL

Plaça del Temple 6
Ciutat Vella ①
+34 963 91 39 55
riverhostelvalencia.com

Extra-wide bunk beds with their own curtains for privacy and cosy common areas to encourage mingling makes this city centre *hostal* a good option for budget stays. In fact, a night in their ten-bed dorm starts from around 16 euro. Activities like pub crawls, bar games and walks take place throughout the week.

445 HI VALENCIA CÁNOVAS

C/ de Ciril Amorós 82
L'Eixample ③
+34 962 06 66 04
hivalenciacanovas.com

Basic but practical, this bed and breakfast is not on the well-trodden tourist path, but it is in one of Valencia's chicest *barrios*, popular with the local office crowd. Double rooms with shared bathrooms start from around 55 euro. The guesthouse even has a rooftop terrace, complete with loungers for basking in the sun.

PLATJA DE LA PATACONA

35 WEEKEND ACTIVITIES

5 perfect plans for
WINE FANS

446 PAGO DE THARSYS
Carretera Nacional III,
km 274
Requena
+34 962 30 33 54
pagodetharsys.com

This 12-hectare vineyard has been practising organic farming for decades, and they've spent even longer refining their cava. They host visitors amongst the vineyards and almond trees in the cosy bodega or beside the lake in a cheerful wooden chalet. Tours complete with three glasses of wine cost just 15 euro.

447 EL CELLER DE PROAVA
C/ de Baix 29
Ciutat Vella ①
+34 963 92 44 63
proavamagazine.com/ el-celler-valencia

It was an ordinary day at work when a builder jammed their pickaxe into this Mediaeval wine store. Left undisturbed for more than 800 years, the time capsule was uncovered and preserved. It's now a curious venue for wine tastings; a quick peek and a chat cost 5 euro, guided tastings 12 euro.

446 PAGO DE THARSYS

448 BODEGA SIERRA NORTE

Diseminado
Diseminados 208
Requena
+34 674 21 90 74
bodegasierranorte.com

In the winemaking region of Requena, this modern bodega invites visitors to the cool tasting room with far-reaching views of the countryside. Join a group for 12 euro, it includes four glasses of wine and cheeses, or just rock up to the enormous terrace and choose from incredibly well-priced bottles.

449 EL CELLER DE LA IBOLA

CV-223 15
Aín
+34 674 50 30 87
elcellerdelaibola.com

Ainhoa and Román set up this tiny winery on the edge of the picture book town of Aín. The patio is a dreamy space, lit with fairy lights and offering views over terracotta-topped *casitas*. On warm evenings, locals come here to listen to jazz and eat locally made charcuterie. There's even a friendly fox that visits.

450 CHE VINS

C/ de Cuba 30
L'Eixample ③
+34 960 70 44 76
chevins.es

Forget stuffy sommeliers, this bright-pink fronted bar in Russafa runs fun tasting events – there's tons to choose from. Quaff wine from the organic, sustainably minded team at Bodegas Clos Cor Ví in Requena with an expert leading the way, or join a vermouth-tasting workshop, which includes four glasses paired with tapas.

5 spectacular
BIKE ROUTES

451 EASY RIDE: JARDÍ DEL TÚRIA

This should be the first destination for anyone let loose on a bike. The River Túria used to run here, but now it's joggers, cyclists and unhurried walkers that flow through the nine-kilometre park. Cycle until you find a nice picnic spot, or refuel at a cafe – Cafetería Kiosko El Río near Alameda metro has a sunny terrace and cold beer.

451 JARDÍ DEL TÚRIA

452 CITY TO BEACH: FROM TORRES DELS SERRANS TO PATACONA

From Jardí del Túria, there are oodles of cycle routes. Try a simple one from the city centre (Torres dels Serrans works) to the indie cafes and sandy beach bars of Patacona. Pass Pont de la Trinitat (the oldest bridge in Valencia), turn off towards Veles e Vents, and follow the seafront cycle path.

453 COUNTRYSIDE: THE VIA XURRA

The Via Xurra is a 16-kilometre route that connects the villages in the northern farmland with the city. Jump on the flat path and whizz past *horchata* fields, sweetly scented orange groves and old *fincas*. The best pit stop is Orxatería Vida, a cafe serving *horchata* in a pretty garden with ducks and peacocks.

454 LONGER BEACH RIDE: EL SALER

From the city centre it's around 14 kilometres to this beach with sand like golden sugar. Use the Jardí del Túria to reach Ciutat de les Arts i les Ciències. On the Assut de l'Or bridge (the side of El Saler shopping centre) there's a bike route – no need to cycle on the busy CV-500 road.

455 TO THE POTTERY PUEBLO: MANISES

This route starts anywhere along Jardí del Túria. Head northeast 12 kilometres, towards a ceramics town full of hand-painted tiles and historic pots. Cycle past the Parc de Capçalera, join the Ruta del Parc Fluvial del Túria and cross the Pont de Manises, leading to the Museu De Ceràmica and Oficina de Turismo.

5 SECLUDED PARKS
for picnics and sunbathing

456 JARDINS DE VIVERS
C/ de Cavanilles
La Saïdia ⑥

This park was the grounds of Palau Reial, a site used by royals since the 11th century and destroyed in 1810 for military strategies. There's an aviary, duck pond with black swans, and a scattering of monuments. Look for the bust of General Elío, legend goes it's placed where he was garrotted in 1822.

457 JARDÍ DE POLIFIL
C/ de la Canal de Navarrés
Campanar ⑤

This secluded garden was inspired by a book called *Sueño de Polífilo*, written by a Valencian priest in 1499. It follows a protagonist on a pilgrimage through a labyrinth of gardens in search of love. Follow in Polífilo's footsteps and walk through winding mazes to traverse laurels, orange trees, cypresses and rosewood.

458 JARDÍ DE MONFORTE

458 JARDÍ DE MONFORTE

C/ de Montforte
El Pla del Real ⑥

This garden is considered one of the best examples of neoclassical parks around. The neon pink tunnel of bougainvillea probably wasn't intended to be a selfie hot spot, but it is. Elsewhere, Italian sculptures recline, like the elegant fountain of Poseidon. The perimeter wall has goat horns embedded in it – nobody knows why.

459 JARDÍ D'AIORA

C/ dels Sants Just i
Pastor 98
Camins al Grau ⑦

With the exception of the playground, it's usually quiet in this park, set away from the city centre but with a convenient metro stop outside. Find the 103-year-old banyan tree in the centre. It was built in 1900 for José and Dolores Ayora, their villa is now a cultural centre run by Universitat Popular.

460 PARC DE CAPÇALERA

Av. Pío Baroja
Campanar ⑤

Found in the old channel of the Túria, this 33-hectare park is criss-crossed with bike paths, wooden walkways and dotted with kids play areas like a big green tapestry. Find the boat-shaped kid's park with slides and climbing walls and a cafe nearby. Feeling romantic? Hire a swan pedalo and hit the lake.

5 amazing
BEACHES

---

461 PLATJA DE LA PATACONA
Alboraia ⑧

Described as the millennial beach of Valencia, Patacona is the furthest beach from the city centre, and draws a diverse crowd for its live music, beach bars, and restaurants. You're just as likely to find brunch and cocktails here as you are paella, and water sports like SUP and surfing are taking off.

462 PLATJA DE LA MALVA-ROSA
Poblats Maritims ⑧

Until around 1848, this was the sole hang-out of fishing families. That was until French botanist Jean Closier arrived. He grew hollyhock (*malvaceae* in Latin, or *alcea rosea*) for his perfume; it's where the beach got its name. Now it's a sporty stretch with volleyball courts and one kilometre of butter-yellow sand.

463 EL SALER
Pobles del Sud

Popular with families and those looking for a (slightly) quieter alternative to the city beaches, El Saler is a white sandy beach with dunes like small mountains. Two restaurants with sea views compete for attention at the entrance – both serve paella and traditional nibbles.

464 PLATJA DOSSEL
Cullera

On a stretch of coast that is generally quite built up, this golden beach has managed to resist too much development, with the exception of the odd building here and there. It means it's a good spot for nature lovers and birdwatchers, the quiet and keen-eyed might see sanderlings and Kentish plovers.

465 PLATJA RACÓ DE LA MAR
(CANET D'EN BERENGUER BEACH)
Canet

Another popular family hang-out, this blue flag beach normally has a lifeguard on watch. There are a few stones near the crystal-clear water, but we'll forgive them. Head to the marina for windsurfing, sailing and kayaking, or stroll on the palm tree promenade, stopping at ice-cream parlours and sun-bleached restaurants.

461 PLATJA DE LA PATACONA

5 WILD SWIMMING
spots and WATERFALLS

466 GORGO DE LA ESCALERA
Anna

The town of Anna is a 50-minute drive from Valencia; it's here that a sign marks the top of the 136 steps down to the waterfall. Cold water shoots into a turquoise pool where people swim or perch on rocks admiring the spectacle. Bring cash: there's a 2-euro entry fee in high season.

467 FUENTE DE LOS BAÑOS
Montanejos

It's just over an hour's drive to these thermal springs surrounded by the mountains of Montanejos. In the 13th century, caliph Zayd Abu Zayd and his harem loved a splash here, he was convinced the water had healing properties. No car? There are lots of day trips that whisk visitors here.

468 LOS CHARCOS DE QUESA
Quesa

It's a fair journey to these pools southwest of Valencia, about an hour and a half by car. The reward? A network of emerald green baths carved into a canyon, one of which has a picturesque waterfall. Cash is required: 1 euro per person and 2 euro per car. Take sandwiches for the shaded picnic benches.

469 PARQUE FLUVIAL
Buñol

This new footpath along the Buñol River has plenty of opportunities for an impulsive paddle. Traverse emerald green pools surrounded by mountain scenery, from Parque de San Luis to Molino Galán. Ask locals about the secret El Paraíso swimming pool. Buñol is also home to the famous La Tomatina festival.

470 LA CUEVA TURCHE
Buñol
*turismolahoya.
buñol.es*

From the car park (there are fines for anyone parking on the road) it's an enjoyable five-minute amble between pine trees to the spectacular 60-metre-tall waterfall. Want to make the most of the journey? Trudge up to the Mirador de la Cueva Turche for rugged views of the rocky landscape.

5 things to do in the
ALBUFERA

---

471 WALK: LA DEVESA AND ESTANY DEL PUJOL

Between the sea and the Albufera (the largest freshwater lake in Spain), there's a network of forest and dunes where the only sound is the wind amongst the reeds and the birds overheard. La Devesa is a wild sandy beach, from here it's a pleasant walk around the artificial lake Estany del Pujol.

472 EAT: EL PALMAR

This sleepy town was built on fishing and rice, and dates back to a Muslim settlement founded in 711 AD. Restaurants specialise in dishes made from produce harvested nearby, like *esgarraet*, rice with duck, and fried eel. After lunch, take a boat tour of the lake and spot herons paddling.

473 BIRD WATCHING: RESERVA NATURAL DEL RACÓ DE L'OLLA

parquesnaturales. gva.es

Grab a pair of binoculars and head to the Racó de l'Olla nature reserve. The retro visitors centre has a look-out tower with sweeping views of the lakes and a cabin where twitchers can set up camp, complete with information on what birds you should be looking for.

474 VISIT RICE FIELDS: MUNTANYETA DELS SANTS

Rice fields are surprisingly beautiful and the best views are from this hill, 27 metres above sea level. The look-out is crowned by the church Ermita dels Benissants de la Pedra, which dates back to 1613. Views change with the seasons; in spring it's a sea of green and in autumn birds shelter in the fields after the harvest.

475 WATER VIEWS: PORT DE CATARROJA

This port is small, with just a few houses and one old-school restaurant, but it is charming. It is a window into old Albufera, where fishing and water was a way of life. Walk the wooden docks, admire the boats, and finish in Casa Baina to try their famous *all i pebre*.

475 PORT DE CATARROJA

The 5 best **S P A S**

476 **CALM & LUXURY**

AT: HOTEL SH
VALENCIA PALACE
Passeig de
l'Albereda 32
El Pla del Real ⑥
+34 962 32 48 12
calmluxury.com

This sixth-floor spa is indoors, but large windows overlooking the Túria make it bright and airy. There's a sauna with spectacular views, a plunge pool and Turkish baths. Massages range from quick foot affairs to full body extravaganzas. Couples can book out the whole thing for 350 euro, complete with a bottle of champagne.

477 **COBRE 29**

AT: HOTEL MELIÁ
Av. de les Corts
Valencianes 52
Benicalap ⑤
+34 961 36 80 60
cobre29.es

Copper is the theme at Cobre, found on the third floor of Meliá hotel. There are a few massages to choose from: Koprum uses copper pebbles, and Aero is a treatment with clay dotted with tiny pieces of copper. Most treatments include a stint in the indoor pool and Valencia residents get 15% off.

478 SPA LAS ARENAS

AT: HOTEL BALNEARIO
LAS ARENAS
C/ d'Eugènia Viñes 22
Poblats Maritims ⑧
+34 963 12 06 62
*hotelvalencia
lasarenas.com/en/spa*

The spa may be the best part of this five-star beachfront hotel, with its secluded outdoor pool and sunbathing area, shielded by palms and banana trees. Thai massages are followed by a jaunt on the wellness circuit, which includes a Scottish shower (read: really cold shower), steam room, ice fountain and aromatherapy.

479 ORIGEN COSMETICS

C/ de l'Arquebisbe
Mayoral 11
Ciutat Vella ②
+34 960 06 40 47
origencosmetics.com

Local vineyard Chozas Carrascal set up this city-centre wine spa. Treatments use the native Bobal grape, high in anti-oxidants, to make moisturisers and oils which they use for massages and facials. At 150 euro per couple, *Ritual Del Enólogo* is the works: massage, wine bath and a glass each of the bodega's best tipple.

480 SPA BODYNA

AT: HOSPES PALAU
DE LA MAR
Av. de Navarro
Reverter 14
L'Eixample ③
+34 963 16 28 84
*hospes.com/en/
palau-mar/spa-
bodyna-valencia*

Found in a 19th-century mansion, this hotel's indoor swimming pool and Jacuzzi is simple and small, but the first-floor treatment rooms are sunny with views of the hotel's courtyard garden. Massages start from around 50 euro, and for 130 two people can get a massage, spa circuit and a three-course dinner.

20 RANDOM FACTS ABOUT VALENCIA

---

5 amazing
MYTHS and LEGENDS

481 THE CAT HOUSE
C/ del Museu 11
Ciutat Vella ①

Don't miss this ankle-high abode with a teeny terracotta-tiled roof. Made by Alfonso Yuste Navarro, it leads to a garden where cats roam freely. It's dedicated to the El Carmen cats of 1094. Legend goes that when El Cid conquered the city in that year he found as many cats as people.

482 THE PRESERVED ARM OF SANT VICENTE
AT: CATEDRAL DE VALÈNCIA
Plaça de la Reina
Ciutat Vella ①
catedraldevalencia.es

Visiting Valencia Cathedral? Look out for a thousand-year-old withered arm. San Vicente Mártir was allegedly killed after refusing to denounce Christianity to the Romans in 304. Despite a tortuous death his left arm miraculously stayed in one piece, and it's displayed here in a bronze cabinet.

483 LA ESTRECHA
Plaça de Lope de Vega 9
Ciutat Vella ②

There's often a tour group outside this building being told that it is the narrowest in Europe. Sadly it's not true. The 107-centimetre-wide façade is just that: a façade. It used to be that small, but since it was knocked through in the 1980s there are no world records here, just a load of fabulous hats by Sombreros Albero.

484 THE DRAGON OF THE PATRIARCA

AT: ESGLÉSIA DEL PATRIARCA
C/ de la Nau 2
Ciutat Vella ②

There's a scaly surprise for visitors to the church on Plaça del Col·legi del Patriarca: an enormous stuffed crocodile coiled on the wall. Some say it's the remains of a 13th-century dragon that lived in the River Túria. Others say it was sent to the church in the 1600s from the viceroy of Peru.

485 PLAÇA DE L'ESPART AND THE POLTERGEIST

Plaça de l'Espart
Ciutat Vella ①

The first registered case of poltergeist in Spain was in Valencia. Bangs and loud noises coming from number 7 (now 5) terrorised the neighbours. So much so that a team of 40 officers cordoned off the area and started an investigation. They found nothing. Must have been a poltergeist, right?

481 THE CAT HOUSE

5 little-known
HISTORICAL SITES

486 MEMORIAL FOR MARGARIDA BORRÀS

AT: MERCAT CENTRAL DE VALÈNCIA

Plaça del Mercat
Ciutat Vella ②

There's a small plaque on Mercat Central dedicated to Margarida Borràs, a transgender woman. Born Miquel, she lived her life as a woman before she was arrested, tortured and hanged in Plaça del Mercat in 1460. The plaque was erected in 2017 in honour of Borràs and all victims of transphobia.

489 PORTAL DE VALLDIGNA

487 THE VOW OF DARKNESS

AT: IGLESIA DE SANTA CATALINA MÁRTIR

Ciutat Vella ②

Between the middle ages and the 18th century, some women took a 'vow of darkness' to show their dedication to God. They were locked in small rooms in the crevices of churches, knowing they would die there. Lots were covered, but some churches in Valencia still have the small barred windows.

488 THE LAST HANGMAN

C/ Estret de la Companyia

Ciutat Vella ②

On this tucked-away street there's a blocked-up door, former home of Valencia's hangman (*el verdugo*), Pascual. Legend goes he fell in love with the last woman publicly garrotted, Josefa. Pascual asked for her to be pardoned. Not only was it declined, he carried out the execution 1896 and was fired shortly after.

489 PORTAL DE VALLDIGNA

C/ del Portal de Valldigna

Ciutat Vella ①

This archway in El Carmen was built in the 1400s to divide the Christians from the Moorish population. They had stayed in the city after the conquest by Jaime I, but were forced outside the old city walls. It was also the site of one of the first printing presses in the Iberian Peninsula.

490 BOMB DAMAGE ON THE TOWN HALL FROM THE CIVIL WAR

Plaça de l'Ajuntament

Ciutat Vella ②

Hundreds walk past the town hall (*ajuntament*) every day, but very few notice the craters. In November 1936 the Popular Front moved the government from Madrid to Valencia, which made the city a target for Franco; spot the bomb damage at street level on the left-hand side of the town hall.

5

MOTIFS and SYMBOLS

that often go unnoticed

---

491 **BAT ON THE COAT OF ARMS OF VALENCIA**

There are a couple of legends that explain the bat in the city's coat of arms. One says that a bat woke up Jaime I to alert him to a surprise invasion by the Moors. A second states that a bat flew into the King's head as he walked into the city after his conquest – he considered it a blessing.

492 **LOS CANECILLOS**
AT: CATEDRAL DE VALÈNCIA
C/ del Palau
Ciutat Vella ①
catedraldevalencia.es

On Valencia Cathedral, the Puerta del Palau has a row of fourteen heads peering out of it. The meaning of these seven men and seven women has been debated, but some say they represent the people who brought 700 women from Lleida to Valencia to be the wives of the first Christian residents.

493 **ORANGES IN THE TRAIN STATION**
AT: ESTACIÓ DEL NORD
C/ de Xàtiva 24
L'Eixample ③

At the Estació del Nord there are countless mosaic oranges, and not just because they look cute: they are a symbol of prosperity, success and agriculture. Spain is the largest producer of citrus fruit in Europe, producing around six million tonnes a year, and Valencia reportedly grows around 70 percent of that.

494 THE PARROT OF MERCAT CENTRAL
AT: MERCAT CENTRAL
DE VALÈNCIA
**Plaça de la Ciutat
de Bruges
Ciutat Vella** ②

There's a talkative character on the
iron and glass roof of Mercat Central:
a huge parrot on the weather vane known
as *Cotorra del Mercat*. It's a nod to the
chatter and gossiping that takes place
in the building below, a good-natured
ribbing not just of the stallholders but
the visitors too.

495 FUENTE DEL TÚRIA
**Plaça de la Verge
Ciutat Vella** ①

There's a relaxed-looking fella in Plaça
de la Verge, part of the elegant bronze
fountain which says more than meets the
eye. Built in 1976, it's a representation
of the River Túria. The guy on top is
Neptune, surrounded by eight women
pouring vases: they represent the eight
canals that water the farmland around
the city.

493 **ORANGES IN THE TRAIN STATION**

5 inspiring **BOOKS** and **WEBSITES** *for further reading*

---

496 ALMUERZOS VALENCIANOS
VICENT MARCO

Almuerzo is not a meal in Valencia, it is a way of life. No one captures this more brilliantly and in so much detail than Vicent Marco in *Almuerzos Valencianos*. It lists the best bars in the area and dives into their fascinating backstories. There's an entire chapter dedicated to bread for goodness' sake.

497 1001 CURIOSIDADES DE LA HISTORIA DE VALENCIA
SALVADOR RAGA NAVARRO

If the entire history of Valencia seems intimidating, Salvador Raga Navarro breaks it down into bite-sized chunks in *1001 Curiosidades de la Historia de Valencia*. It's neatly diced into chapters, from interesting streets to fascinating characters to dark histories. Key words are highlighted for readers in a rush.

498 EL TIPO QUE NUNCA CENA EN CASA

eltipoquenunca cenaencasa.com

Food reviews can be a bore, but this sparky copy is always light-hearted and peppered with jokes; they're a joy to read. Working anonymously, El Tipo Que Nunca Cena en Casa (the guy who never eats at home) goes to well-known and off-the-beaten-path spots to find the best no-nonsense grub.

499 GUÍA HEDONISTA

valenciaplaza.com/ guiahedonista

The restaurant and bar section of Valencia Plaza is well informed and especially useful for visitors in need of decent restaurants or up-to-the-minute food news and interviews. Read to get the lowdown on everything from new Cava festivals and interviews with local food legends.

500 LA VALENCIA ETERNA
DAVID HERRERA

Take a mindful and meandering walk through the city with this fascinating history book. Using modern points of reference, David Herrera dives into deep and forgotten stories about Valencia's historic streets, *plaças* and landmarks. The time and work that went into writing it are palpable.

INDEX

COLOPHON

EDITING *and* COMPOSING — Lucy Lovell

GRAPHIC DESIGN — Joke Gossé and doublebill.design

PHOTOGRAPHY — Paula G. Furió

COVER IMAGE — Mercat de Russafa (secret 190)

The addresses in this book have been selected after thorough independent research by the author, in collaboration with Luster Publishing. The selection is solely based on personal evaluation of the business by the author. Nothing in this book was published in exchange for payment or benefits of any kind.

The author and the publisher have made every effort to obtain permission for all illustrations and to list all copyright holders. Interested parties are requested to contact the publisher.

D/2024/12.005/3

ISBN 978 94 6058 3605

NUR 512

© 2024 Luster Publishing, Antwerp
lusterpublishing.com – THE500HIDDENSECRETS.COM
info@lusterpublishing.com

Printed in Italy by Printer Trento.